TH1NK REFERENCE
COLLECTION

the bible

THINK FOR YOURSELF ABOUT WHAT'S INSIDE

Written by General Editor Mark Tabb

D1502596

TH1NK
P.O. Box 35001
Colorado Springs, Colorado 80935

TH1NK is an imprint of NavPress.

TH1NK and the TH1NK logo are registered trademarks of NavPress. Absence of ® in connection with marks of NavPress or other parties does not indicate an absence of registration of those marks.

ISBN 1-57683-956-7

Cover design by Arvid Wallen
Creative Team: Nicci Hubert, Karen Lee-Thorp, Erika Hueneke, Kathy Mosier, Bob Bubnis

The Bible : think for yourself about what's inside / written by general editor Mark Tabb.
    p. cm. -- (TH1NK reference collection)
  Includes bibliographical references.
  ISBN 1-57683-956-7
  1. Bible--Introductions. I. Tabb, Mark A. II. Series.
  BS475.3.B459 2006
  220.6'1--dc22
                           2006006969

Printed in the United States of America

1 2 3 4 5 6 7 8 9 10 / 10 09 08 07 06

Contents

About the TH1NK
REFERENCE COLLECTION

The TH1NK REFERENCE COLLECTION isn't an ordinary set of reference books. Like all of the books in the TH1NK line, we wrote these books for students. That doesn't mean we inserted some hip language into an otherwise dry, boring book to try to make it sound with it and cool, dude. Instead, we built these books on a couple of assumptions about you.

First, we knew you want honest representations of various points of view. Although all the books in the REFERENCE COLLECTION are written from an evangelical Christian position, we didn't dismiss all other viewpoints. Instead, we wrote these books in such a way that those holding different worldviews and theological perspectives would be able to read these books and say, *Yes, this gives a good outline of what I and others believe.* To assure theological balance, all of the books in this collection have been reviewed by a panel of scholars from various theological perspectives and academic fields (see page 271 for a list of those scholars).

We also believed you are able to draw your own conclusions. Whether the question regards what Buddhists believe or whether Christians can lose their salvation, we didn't connect all the dots for you. Each book presents several perspectives. You will have to take the next step on your own and figure out what you believe and why you believe it. Our goal is to do more than answer questions. The TH1NK REFERENCE COLLECTION is designed to make you think through your own beliefs and convictions, as well as those of others.

Finally, we assumed you want something more than a place to turn for answers to your questions about Islam or Psalm 119 or the role of women in the church. That's why we designed these books to be read, not just used for research. You can read them from cover to cover. Along the way, you will find that these books not only dispense information but also entertain you and challenge you and the way you see your world.

Mark Tabb
General Editor

Introduction

Anytime you go someplace you've never been, it's always nice to have a seasoned traveler come alongside and help you get the most out of your visit. For most people, the Bible is an unfamiliar place. That's why we wrote this book for you: as a tour guide. Think of us as a friend riding along with you as you journey through the Bible. We're here to point out things you might otherwise overlook as well as answer some of your questions and keep you on track when you start feeling lost and overwhelmed. This book is by no means an exhaustive resource for all of your questions about the Bible. Instead, we are here to help you do something too few people ever do: Read the Bible for yourself, and think through what you've read. We've even provided a chapter-by-chapter breakdown of the books of the Bible, which, if you follow it, will take you through the Bible in about a year.

WHAT IS IT?
Before diving into the Bible, we need to cover some of the basics, and nothing is more basic than this question: What is the Bible? The word *bible* is simply a transliteration (that is, a word that was not translated into another language but transferred into it) of the Greek word that means "book." We use it to refer to any book that contains indispensable information. The "birdwatcher's bible" refers to a book no self-respecting birdwatcher should be without, while the "shooter's bible" tells gun enthusiasts everything they must know about firearms.

The Bible is the original indispensable book. It was written by more than forty men over a period of more than a thousand years, beginning three thousand years ago. But what sets the Bible apart isn't its age, but its divine quality. When the men who wrote the Bible grabbed a pen and started writing, they didn't just pull words out of the air. Peter said, "Above all, you must understand that no prophecy in Scripture ever came from the prophets themselves or because they wanted to prophesy. It was the Holy Spirit who moved the prophets to speak from God" (2 Peter 1:20-21). This means God worked in the minds and spirits of the Bible's authors so they wrote precisely what he wanted written. Each book still reflects the personality of the human author. That doesn't take away from its inspiration. God chose particular people to be the authors of his Word. He made them, designing their personalities and putting them through unique life circumstances, all of which worked together to produce the volumes he wanted in print. When we pick up this book, we hold the literal Word of God. The actor Stephen Baldwin has perhaps the best answer for those who think this is impossible: "I think if God can create the universe he can write a book."[1]

Because God is ultimately the author of the Bible, it is completely trustworthy and true. His book is as reliable as he is. This means when the Bible says Jesus raised the dead back to life, he actually did it. If you could build a time machine and go back to the moment they rolled the stone away from Lazarus's tomb, you would hear Jesus tell him to get up with your own ears. And if you pressed your way through the crowd, you would see Lazarus, still wrapped up in burial cloths like a mummy, come walking out just as surely as you could watch John Hancock scribble his name on the Declaration of Independence if you could travel back to July 4, 1776.

Although the Bible is completely true, that doesn't mean some parts won't leave you scratching your head going, "Huh?" You won't have to wait long for some of these "huh?" moments. God arranged the Bible in such a way that you get hit with the biggest ones in the first eleven chapters of Genesis. Check it out for yourself. Genesis 1 says God created light on day 1, sky and seas on day 2, and dry land and plants on day 3. But, and this will really blow your mind, he didn't create the sun, moon, and stars until day 4. If you don't ask yourself, *How on earth is that possible?* then you aren't paying attention. Genesis also says people lived seven, eight, even nine hundred years in the early days of human history. How is that possible? No one knows. However, our inability to understand how God did something does not mean the Bible is in error. This is where faith comes in. Believing in the absolute truthfulness of the Bible means believing that when and if all the facts come in, the Bible will be shown to be correct. When it comes to things like the lifespan of people prior to Noah's flood or miracles like Moses turning the Nile River into blood, we may never know how God did it. The important thing is, we know he did, without waiting for an explanation before we believe.

The Bible's divine nature also means we must obey it. This should go without saying. After all, what could possibly be more obvious than knowing we ought to do what God tells us to do since he is, in fact, God? That's like telling you it would be a good idea to cash your paycheck or that you shouldn't climb over the fence surrounding the tiger pit at the zoo. The authority of the Bible should be just as obvious. God, the Creator of the entire universe, the One who scooped up some dirt and made the human race, the One who designed you and laid out your life before you were ever born, has written a book. In that book he tells you how you should live the life he designed. And he promises to change your life when you do what that book says. Call me crazy, but I think he just may know what he's talking about.

The Bible will introduce you to a new life system that will change everything about you. If you let it, it will reshape your values, your priorities, and the entire direction of your life. You will find commands in it and verses that tell you to do this or to not do that, but it has much more. Reading through the Bible will give you a whole new perspective on the world around you. This is called a biblical worldview, which simply means the Bible becomes the lens through which you interpret reality, as God's perspective becomes your own.

YEAH, BUT WHAT IS IT?

The Bible is the indispensable book sent to us from God himself. But when we start to read this divine, authoritative, completely true book, we still don't know exactly what we are getting ourselves into. Is it the textbook for God 101, all the information about God you ever need to know? Is it the place to run for answers to all your questions about eternity? Some people call it the owner's manual for the human soul. Others see it as a treasure chest where we go to uncover pearls of truth to carry with us throughout the day. A recent television commercial referred to it as the instruction book for life. More than one pastor has held up a Bible and called it the rulebook for life. Do any of these really describe the Bible? Even if they don't, they describe the way most of us approach it. Maybe that's why reading it often feels like such a chore.

Think about it. When was the last time you curled up with a good textbook? As soon as a semester ends, most of us sell our textbooks back to the college bookstore. If we do keep some, we never go back and read them for fun. Not if we're normal. Nor do we sit down and read our usual sources for answers to questions and problems for pleasure. Most computer programs come equipped with a "help" section we access by pressing F1. Do you ever press F1 for recreational reading? I didn't think so. And when was the last time you read the owner's manual for your car? Do you even know where it is? How often do you consult the instructions to putting anything together or the rules to Monopoly? Thinking of the Bible as a treasure chest filled with pearls of truth doesn't work either. Open the first page. Is it put together like any other collection of pithy sayings? No, not even close.

SO WHAT IS THIS BOOK WE CALL THE BIBLE?

The first line in the first book gives us a clue. The Bible starts off, "In the beginning God. . . ." Whatever else this book may be, we know its central character is God. As you continue reading, you find God isn't described as some scientist would describe him, nor are all his character qualities cataloged like a theologian might do. Instead, as you read, you encounter God. He speaks and creates the world. Then he makes people and places them in the world. Yet God isn't far off from these people. He carries on conversations with them and spends time with them. Apparently that isn't enough for the people. They turn their backs on God and ignore what he says. And that's just the beginning.

This book starts off reading less like an encyclopedia or a textbook or an owner's manual than it does like a story. And the story keeps going as you continue turning the pages. Through the first five books, on through Joshua and Judges and Samuel and Kings, and into the Prophets, the storyline continues to unfold. Even in the parts where the plotline seems to stop, you can still hear it. The book of Psalms is more than a collection of poems and songs. Each one expresses the heart cry of people in the middle of the unfolding drama of the story of God. I keep looking for something that approaches a God encyclopedia or a section filled with answers to all the critics' questions, but they're nowhere to be found. Instead, I find a true story that unfolds over the course of thousands of years. A story about God.

But what else would we expect to find? When you stand back and look at the Bible as a whole, you find one uniform story unfolding across its sixty-six books. Every part, every book, every psalm, every proverb, every letter, every prophecy, every law—all of it fits together to tell one story, the story of God. The Old Testament tells the first part of the story, and the New gives us part two. This story contains all the key elements you would expect to find in a great novel. One plotline goes from beginning to end, a plotline God has written not only in the Bible, but also across the pages of history. Within this plotline you find multifaceted characters and plot complications. Themes unfold across the storylines that help us understand the characters and plot. The various books within the Bible contain different writing styles and types of literature. Of course you find narratives, but you also find poetry and songs and proverbs and prophecies and letters. Some of the books talk about what happened, a few point to events that haven't yet taken place. All work together to tell God's story. But this true story isn't like any other ever written. We not only read it, we become a part of the drama.

So what is the Bible? It is the ultimate story, God's story. And what should you do with a good story? Read it, of course.

DISCOVERING THE STORY

Stephen King once said that every good story begins with a question. The Bible, however, doesn't begin with a question. It begins with a statement: "In the beginning God. . . ." Yet this statement prompts a question in everyone who reads it, a question that is the single most important issue for every human being who has ever lived: Who is God?

The answer to this question unfolds through God's story, beginning with the Old Testament. The word *testament* means "covenant." A covenant is a binding agreement between two parties that obligates them to do certain things for one another. It's stronger than a contract. Think of wedding vows or a treaty between two nations. The Old Testament contains the covenants God made before the coming of Jesus (and tells what happened when God's people broke their vows), while the New Testament describes the covenant he made through his Son, a covenant that replaced all those that came before.

In the Old Testament God creates the world and hands it to the crowning point of his creation, human beings. The first two people, however, want something bigger and better. They want to be like God. Their disobedience separates the human race from God, plunging all of their descendants into spiritual darkness. Before sin enters the world, there is no question as to who God is. Afterward, the human heart becomes so dark and cold that no one knows. But God loves people too much to leave them in the dark forever. He reaches out to them to reestablish a relationship with them. However, this raises another question: How can sinful people live in the presence of a holy God?

These two questions drive the plot of the Old Testament. By the time you reach the end, you wonder if anyone can ever find the answers. In spite of all of God's efforts to reveal himself to the human race, people continue to run after sin instead of God. Even the people God selects as his own chosen people worship gods made of wood and stone as often as they worship the God in heaven. Can anything be done to set things right between God and people? The answer to this question leads us to the New Testament. God reveals himself in a way he never has before, answering once and for all the question of who he might be. He does this through his Son, Jesus, God made flesh.

The best way to see all this unfold is to begin with the Old Testament, reading in the order in which the books appear in the Hebrew Bible.[2] I know, here comes the first "Uhhh, what are you talking about?" The order of the Old Testament books in the typical Bible you pull off the shelf at a Christian bookstore isn't the same as in the days of Jesus. Jews in the time of Christ divided the Old Testament into three sections: the Law, the Prophets, and the Writings.

The Law consists of five books: Genesis, Exodus, Leviticus, Numbers, and Deuteronomy. As the name suggests, they contain God's Law for his people embedded in a story about his relationship with them. Genesis tells how God creates the universe and the human race. It goes on to tell of his selection of a man and his wife, Abraham and Sarah, to grow into a nation through whom God will make himself known to the entire world. The rest of the books of the Law pick up the story after the descendants of these two people spend four hundred years living in Egypt, where they have become slaves. God sets them free and takes them to a land he promises to give them forever. Some of their descendants still live in that land today. Before God plants this nation in the land, he gives them detailed instructions for living in a close relationship with him.

The Prophets are made up of twenty-one books: Joshua, Judges, 1 and 2 Samuel, 1 and 2 Kings, Isaiah, Jeremiah, Ezekiel, Hosea, Joel, Amos, Obadiah, Jonah, Micah, Nahum, Habakkuk, Zephaniah, Haggai, Zechariah, and Malachi. The last twelve are grouped together and called The Book of the Twelve. We know them today as the Minor Prophets, because the books are shorter than the other prophetic books. Joshua through 2 Kings are called the Former Prophets, for they tell the story of God's people after they move into the land God promised to give them. These books tell us *what* happened to God's nation of Israel, with a focus on those who speak for God in each generation. Isaiah through Malachi are known as the Latter Prophets. They cover the same historical period, but they tell us *why* Israel's history played out as it did.

The third group of books, the Writings, consists of Psalms, Job, Proverbs, Ruth, Song of Solomon, Ecclesiastes, Lamentations, Esther, Daniel, Ezra, Nehemiah, and 1 and 2 Chronicles. Some of these books are poetry, others contain songs. Ruth, Esther, and Daniel through 2 Chronicles tell stories. All thirteen books cover the same historical period as the Prophets, and all share a common characteristic. They show *how* people of faith responded both to the events around them and to God.[3]

Reading the Old Testament in this order not only allows you to see God's story unfold in a way you have never seen before, it also sets the stage for the New Testament. First and Second Chronicles, the last two books in the Hebrew Bible, look forward to God doing something new in the lives of his people who have suffered so long. Yet you come to the end unsure of what that new work might be. That is, until you turn the page and read the first page of the New Testament. Matthew begins by recounting Abraham's descendants, much like the genealogies of 1 Chronicles at the end of the Old Testament. He then shows God's ultimate purpose in calling Abraham as he tells the story of the birth of Jesus, the long-awaited Messiah. Finally, all of the questions of the Old Testament are about to be answered.

CONVERSATIONS WITH GOD

Reading God's story should be an interactive experience. Start your reading with prayer, and continue to talk to God as you read his Word. Listen for what each passage says about God, what it says about people, and how the two go together. Ask questions and dig deeper. Keep a notebook handy to record your thoughts. It can help you listen as God speaks. Again, we're reading a true story about real people in real situations. Put yourself in their positions. What do you think they felt and thought and feared? Could you have responded to God in the way they did? Keeping these kinds of questions at the forefront of your mind will help you truly immerse yourself in this story.

A final word of warning before you dive into the Bible: Some of what you will read will surprise you or trouble you or make you drop the Book and say, "What's *that* doing in the Bible?" God's story is much messier than the *VeggieTales* reenactments would lead you to believe. As you read, you will come across truths that will bring you comfort and others that will cause you to call the way you live your life into question. Expect to get excited over good news and to be made uncomfortable, and at times angry, by what sounds like bad news. You may even find yourself talking back to a page of the Bible saying, "I don't like this *one bit*!" Remember, the Bible is the story of a holy God reaching down to people who tell him to get lost. It reveals the true nature of the universe along with the real condition of the human heart. Because every word of it is true, how could we expect it to be all sunshine and puppies and daisies and warm fuzzies, when the world in which we live is anything but?

And now it's time for the tour to begin. Grab your Bible and let's go. We'll start in the books of the Law. These books set the stage for everything that follows. Then, in the Former Prophets, we'll discover how well God's people did in trying to live close to him. Next, we'll hear God's comments on that sorry story in the Latter Prophets. The first part of our journey ends with the Writings, as we listen to people struggling to live for God in a difficult world. The key question that runs through each of these major divisions of the Hebrew Bible — *How can sinful people live in an intimate relationship with a holy God?* — is never really answered. That's why there's part two of the story, the New Testament.

1

The Law

Genesis, Exodus, Leviticus,
Numbers, Deuteronomy

AUTHOR
Moses

WHEN WERE THESE BOOKS WRITTEN?
During the forty years Israel wandered around in the wilderness, around 1400 BC.

WHAT ARE THEY ABOUT?
These five books cover the story of God from the creation of the world to the moment right before the people of Israel walk into the Promised Land (around 1400 BC). No other section of the Bible covers such a wide span of history. The section gets its name from the central feature of the five books: God's Law as given to Moses. The Law itself begins with the

Ten Commandments in Exodus 20 and stretches through to the end of Deuteronomy. However, the section doesn't read like a legal document. Instead, the Law is interspersed with the story of God choosing a people, then leading them to a land he has prepared for them. It is the foundation for everything that follows in the Bible.

Genesis

Plot: The book tells the story of creation, both of the universe and of the nation of Israel, the people through whom God chooses to reveal himself to the world. What will God do when the people he created to know him and love him reject him instead?

Key characters: God, Adam and Eve, Noah, Abraham and Sarah, Isaac, Jacob, Joseph

Turning points in the story: Genesis 3; 12

Exodus

Plot: Exodus tells how the people of Israel become slaves in Egypt and how God sets them free. Their time in Egypt allows them to grow into a nation of several million. The book also records the Ten Commandments and the first part of God's Law that governs how people can live in a relationship with him.

Key characters: Moses, Aaron, Pharaoh, the people of Israel

Turning point in the story: Exodus 12

Leviticus

Plot: Leviticus picks up where Exodus ends. It was written while the people of Israel were camped around Mount Sinai, the place where God gave them the Law. Leviticus primarily focuses on how people can worship God. It details the sacrifices necessary to remove the offense of sin so that a relationship with God is possible.

Key characters: Moses, Aaron, Nadab, Abihu

Turning point in the story: Leviticus 10

Numbers

Plot: The book gets its name from the two censuses Moses takes of Israel in the wilderness. God takes the people to the Promised Land, but the people don't believe they can conquer the people who already live there in order to obtain it. So God sentences that generation to wander around in the desert until another generation grows up to take their place, a generation who believes God can do what he said.

Key characters: Moses, the twelve spies including Caleb and Joshua, Korah, Balaam

Turning point in the story: Numbers 13

Deuteronomy

Plot: These are Moses' final words to the people he led for more than forty years as they stand poised to enter the Promised Land. The book gets its name from two Greek words that mean "the second giving of the Law." As its name implies, Moses gives the Law to the people a second time, telling them both how they are supposed to live in the land they are about to enter and how to live in the presence of a holy God.

Key characters: Moses, the new generation of Israel

Turning point in the story: Deuteronomy 34

Genesis

The first generation always has the greatest influence over any movement or organization. This is especially true of the human race. The first generation opened the door through which every generation since has passed. We find both the very best and the very worst about ourselves in these chapters. This is perhaps the most important book in the entire Bible for understanding God, the state of the world, and human nature. Every theme found in the rest of Scripture first appears in Genesis. From who we are, to the depth of our depravity, to the power of God and the wonder of his grace, it can all be found here.

Genesis covers the largest span of time of all the books of the Bible, from the dawn of creation until Jacob and his family settle in Egypt (around 1800 BC). Some of the Bible's most memorable characters are found here, including Adam and Eve, Noah, and Abraham, Isaac, and Jacob, the forefathers of the ethnic Jewish people and the spiritual fathers of all who believe.

Genesis 1–3

The Creation account in Genesis doesn't tell us *how*, but *who*. God designs all that is and speaks it into existence. The only thing he doesn't speak into existence is you and me. In Genesis 2, God scoops up some dirt, shapes it into a man, pulls the man to his lips, and breathes into him the breath of life. He crafts man and woman in his own image, able to create, rule, and love. Their nature as God's image-bearers separates them from all the rest of creation.

These first few chapters also introduce us to the great dilemma that runs through the Bible. God creates people to know him, to love him, to enjoy an intimate relationship with him as they enjoy the world he places them in. But he also gives them a choice about this relationship. They aren't robots programmed to love God. It doesn't take long for them to choose. Adam and Eve, the first man and woman, weigh their options and decide they would rather be like God than take a position of subservience. As a result, they die spiritually and later physically. Since sin cannot exist in the presence of a holy God, the Lord drives them away from himself. How can they ever be brought back? People have dug the gulf that separates God and mankind. How will God reestablish an intimate relationship with people who choose sin over him, and why would he? And how will people who fall in love with sin the day they first taste it ever be able to live without it?

Genesis 4–7

Genesis 6 says, "The sons of God saw the beautiful women of the human race and took any they wanted as their wives." The offspring of these relationships are referred to as giants who became the heroes of the legends of old. Does this mean angels intermarry with human beings and produce some sort of angelic hybrid superhumans? No. Jesus says angels don't marry; that is, they are incapable of procreation (Matthew 22:30). If the "sons of God" in Genesis 6 aren't angels, the phrase probably refers to godly men from the line of Seth, who abandon all godly standards and marry whomever they wish. This is one of those passages where an exact understanding is not completely possible. The point, though, is clear. The human race plunges itself into the depths of sin, with sexual sin at the forefront. This makes God lose patience with the human race.

The identity of the giants is easier to pin down. The term translated "giants" in the New Living Translation literally means "the fallen ones" or "those who fall upon others," that is, with violence. It refers to the men of renown, violent men who dominated all others. They are physically huge, especially in comparison with the average person. However, giant doesn't mean the Jolly Green Giant. Think in terms of Shaq compared with the average human being. Goliath, the Philistine hero whom David kills in 1 Samuel, is nine feet tall in an era when the average Israelite is a little more than five feet tall. A similar ratio probably applies here in Genesis.

Genesis 8–11

The key to understanding the tower of Babel story lies in 11:4, "Let's build a great city . . . a monument to our greatness." The tower is both a monument to the power of human ability and a means of uniting the entire human race. Why is this bad? They are united in exerting their greatness in opposition to God. Remember what just happened in the beginning of human history? People went from bad to worse and digressed into a state of total wickedness. If God leaves the people of Babel to themselves, history will immediately repeat itself.

Genesis 12–15

The story of the Flood shows how there are no limits to human depravity. Yet no matter how bad people become, God still loves them. His plan for them remains. He longs to bring them back to himself. We see this in the mercy God shows when he saves the human race through Noah and the ark. Sadly, tasting God's mercy and grace doesn't change the pattern. After the Flood, people don't change. Instead, they pool their efforts and attempt to become like God, which sounds very much like the Garden of Eden all over again. Now what will God do? How can he establish a loving, intimate relationship with humankind, while still maintaining his justice and holiness? Will he ever find anyone on the earth whose heart will be completely his? The answers to these questions unfold in the next phase of the story, which introduces a man and his wife named Abram and Sarai.

Genesis 16–19

Why are Abram and Sarai so important to God's story and his plan of salvation for the human race? From these two people, God will make a whole new nation, a new race of people, through whom he will reveal himself to the entire world. God's plan is to reveal himself to Abram and his descendants, both in actions and words. Abram and his descendants are then to tell the rest of the world about him. Enough generations have passed from Adam to Noah to show that no one will come to God on his own. Through Abram and Sarai and their descendants, God will now reveal himself in an unmistakable way. His goal is more than to get people to believe he exists. God wants all people to know him intimately and personally. Of course, this is impossible as long as we remain in our sin. More on that plot complication later. The rest of Genesis records the beginning of the nation descended from Abram and Sarai. There's only one problem. They're both old and childless. How can God build a nation from a man pushing a hundred and an old woman near ninety?

Genesis 20–26

The story takes an unusual turn in chapter 22. At long last a child is born to Abraham and Sarah (Abram and Sarai renamed).

This child fulfills God's promises to them. Now Abraham is supposed to sacrifice this child. What on earth is God thinking? For more insight into this episode, see Hebrews 11:17-19. As you read these chapters, put yourself in the drama. How would you see God if you were Sarah? Or Hagar? Or Ishmael? Or Abraham? Put yourself in Isaac's place as he lies on top of the pile of wood waiting for his dad to kill him. How would this episode change your understanding of God?

Abraham sometimes pales in comparison with his son Isaac. As you read about his life, think about what he goes through when his father is about to sacrifice him in chapter 22. Abraham is more than one hundred years old. Isaac is a young man, probably in his early teens. If he wanted to, he could easily stop his father. He doesn't. Think about the faith he has to exercise, both in his father and in God. Keep this in mind as you read about how he obeys when God speaks.

Genesis 27–35

Here Jacob steals his brother Esau's birthright and blessing, then runs for his life. Jacob knows sticking around greatly increases his odds of an unfortunate and potentially fatal accident. But his fear of Esau doesn't change Jacob's modus operandi. He keeps on dealing from the bottom of the deck in his interaction both with people and with God. And here's the really strange twist: This is the guy God chooses to be the vessel through whom the tribes of Israel will be born. Jacob is not the picture of godliness. His story introduces us to something mysterious and far beyond human comprehension, something we can only call grace.

As you read about Jacob and his sons, remember the Bible records the real lives of its characters. By doing so, God does not sanction everything they do. Jacob shows God works in and through these people in spite of what they do and who they are. His story magnifies the wonder of God's mercy and grace.

Genesis 36–39

Chapters 38–39 show the incredible contrast in character between Joseph and his brothers. Notice how Joseph and his brother Judah respond when tempted. Look at how each one handles sexual sin. One goes looking for the opportunity to give in; the other runs away when temptation is forced upon him. Could two men be any more different?

Genesis 40–50

These chapters show God's incredible power and sovereignty, especially when it appears outwardly that he is far away. What hope would anyone have if Joseph had not been sold into slavery by his brothers and later put into prison unjustly by Potiphar? Also, how desperate must Pharaoh be to listen to a foreign prisoner?

As the story unfolds, it becomes clear that God wants Jacob and his family to move to Egypt. Why? The answer lies in Genesis 43:32. The Egyptians despise the Hebrews. They won't even eat in the same room with them. Once Jacob's family moves to Egypt, there isn't much chance that they'll absorb into the local population. No Egyptian wants to intermarry with them. God isolates this group of seventy people until they grow into a large and distinct people. The only question will then be, after living in Egypt for a few hundred years, why would these people ever want to leave?

BEFORE YOU MOVE ON . . .

By the end of Genesis, you have the makings of the new nation through whom God will make himself known to the entire world. Yet a couple of problems stand in the way. First, there are only seventy people. And they live a long way from the land God promised to give them. Joseph is dead, but no one has hauled his body back to Canaan. They have put him in a coffin. Notice, they don't bury him. He's in a box, as though he doesn't want to settle for living in Egypt even though he is dead. Joseph protected Israel's descendants from the Egyptians. What will happen now that he's dead? And how can seventy people grow into a nation? And what will happen to the promises God made to Abraham since his descendants have put down roots in Egypt, not the Promised Land?

Exodus

When Pharaoh invited Joseph's father and family to move to Egypt, he told them, "Don't worry about your belongings, for the best of all the land of Egypt shall be yours" (Genesis 45:20). In addition, Joseph made sure his extended family settled in Goshen, a fertile area perfect for raising sheep, cattle, and oxen.

After four hundred years of living there, the group of seventy has grown to several million, with more than six hundred thousand men twenty years of age and older. What can possibly motivate not just a handful of people, but the entire nation, to pull up stakes and move to a land they've never seen? Life has to be so bad, so horrible, they would all rather risk death than stay where they are. And that is exactly what you discover is everyday life in Egypt for Jacob's descendants. Four hundred years go by between the end of Genesis and the beginning of Exodus, approximately the same amount of time that passed from the time the last book of the Old Testament was written to the birth of Jesus. During this time, life takes some unexpected twists that prepare God's people for what he plans to do next.

Exodus 1–5

Why does God threaten to kill Moses? To understand the answer, you need to think in terms of God's plan for Moses' life. Leading the Jews to freedom constitutes only a small part of God's purpose. God also plans to give his people his Law through Moses. Up to this time, the Hebrews know only two commands from God: Keep the Sabbath (Genesis 2:3), and circumcise all males (Genesis 17:9-14). How can Moses deliver God's Law to God's people when he hasn't kept the small portion of the Law he already knows? Even after the Lord appeared to him in the burning bush, Moses didn't correct this oversight by getting circumcised. If Moses the lawgiver doesn't take God and his Word seriously, why will anyone else?

Why doesn't God tell Moses to ask for the slaves' freedom? Read the story carefully. Moses asks Pharaoh to allow the Hebrews to go on a three-day journey into the wilderness to worship the Lord (5:1). He never says anything about leaving and never coming back. To understand the answer you must also see the situation from God's perspective. God asks for a three-day worship trip, but once he completely destroys Egypt, Pharaoh wants them gone forever. Setting them free is Pharaoh's idea. God doesn't switch the price tags. Instead, once he shows his might to Egypt, the Egyptians don't want to mess with him or his people.

Exodus 6–8

God's plagues have a dual purpose. First, they break the Egyptians and set his people free. But the Egyptians aren't the only audience. The Israelites aren't exactly the godliest of people. Many of them worship the Egyptian gods. Moses knows if he goes to the Israelites and declares, "God sent me," they will reply, "Which one?" Therefore, the plagues on Egypt are all aimed at showing the Israelites that the Lord alone is God. Perhaps that is why the first plague directly targets the Egyptians' favorite god: the river of life, the Nile. Note also how the first three plagues affect the entire land, including Goshen, where the Israelites live. But beginning with the fourth plague, gnats, God makes a distinction between the Israelites and the Egyptians. Egypt suffers, Israel is spared. God does this to show both the Israelites and the Egyptians that these aren't random, natural events.

Exodus 9–12

Verse 9:12 raises the question: Does Pharaoh have a choice? The verse says God hardens his heart, making him even more stubborn. Is that fair? Does God force him to act as he does? Read Romans 1:24,28 and 9:17-18 for the answers. Part of God's judgment is turning people over to the choices they make. God makes Pharaoh even more stubborn as a way of sealing his fate. He raises up this particular man for the express purpose of putting someone so stubborn on Egypt's throne that he won't surrender until the entire nation is destroyed and every false god discredited. Is God being fair by doing this? Very. And that's why this bothers most of us. Fair means giving someone what he deserves. When it comes to punishment, we don't want fairness. We prefer mercy, at least for ourselves. But Pharaoh doesn't receive mercy. God gives him what he deserves, a frightening prospect indeed.

Exodus 13–20

How can the Israelites go from singing God's praises on the day they cross the Red Sea (chapter 15) to complaining that he's sent them into the desert to die less than a month later (16:3)? Before we throw rocks at them, we need to ask ourselves, *How often do I find myself doubting God and complaining about the way he is running my life?* We aren't as different from them as we would like to think.

Why do the Israelites take such an indirect route through the wilderness? God could take them on a direct and speedy route to the Promised Land. He could, but he knows they aren't ready (13:17). Taking possession of the land will be a matter not of military superiority, but of faith. Just as God fought their battles against the Egyptians, he will fight against every other foe they face. Now, during their time in the wilderness, God wants to teach them to trust him. He also needs to give them his Law, by which they can live in a close relationship with him.

Finally, Jethro's statement in 18:11 is the key verse for understanding not only the plagues in Egypt but also all the battles that lie in Israel's future. Every battle is a battle between gods. When Israel fights against another nation, the question isn't which god is strongest, but which god is real. The Lord wants every person to come to the same realization that strikes Jethro as he says, "Now I know that the LORD is greater than all other gods, for he did this to those who had treated Israel arrogantly" (NIV).

Exodus 21–24
As you read the Law, beginning with the Ten Commandments, notice how practical it is. The instructions God gives the people are to govern their everyday lives. That's why so many laws focus on how to get along with one another. Others deal with matters of cleanliness and disease. The first set of regulations immediately following the Ten Commandments focuses on rules governing slavery. They sound strange to our modern ears, and we wonder why God would even address this without simply condemning it outright. But to people who have just spent hundreds of years in slavery, this topic is probably front and center in their minds.

Exodus 25–31
The tabernacle is more than an ancient equivalent of a church building. It's the place where God makes his presence known to

the people in a tangible way. That's why the Greek equivalent of the word *tabernacle* is used in the New Testament to describe Jesus' coming to earth. This movable structure reflects God's greatness and holiness and glory. The building instructions are also practical. After all, this tent has to last a very long time. That's why the roof is made of skins that repel water with a layer of goat's hair to insulate it.

In addition to providing a place for people to meet with him, God also gives them worship leaders who will lead them to himself. Don't think in terms of the praise teams we have in churches today. Instead, these worship leaders are selected to represent the people to God. That's why the rules for who can be priests, how they must conduct themselves, and even what they can wear are so important. The priests go into the tabernacle and stand before God to plead the people's case. They have to be holy, just as God is holy.

Everything in this section is important, but that doesn't mean it makes for stimulating reading. Don't worry if you find this more than a little boring. You aren't alone. Most people find this part of the Law less than exciting. Skimming is not a sin.

Exodus 32–33

How can Aaron, Moses' own brother and the man who spoke for Moses to Pharaoh, now stand in front of a golden cow and say, "O Israel, these are the gods who brought you out of Egypt!"? And how can these people who watched the plagues destroy Egypt, and who walked through the Red Sea, and who ate manna every day, worship a golden cow instead of the Lord? And here's the real kicker: How can God take these people back and even make Aaron his high priest?

Exodus 34–40

Exodus 34:14 in the NLT captures the reason why God goes to all the trouble of setting apart this people for himself: "You must worship no other gods, but only the LORD, for he is a God who is passionate about his relationship with you." All of the laws and rules and regulations may make God appear very narrow-minded. In truth, they show how wide a canyon our sin digs between us and God and why God reaches across it.

Leviticus

Living in the wonder of God's grace poured out through Jesus, we often take our access to God for granted. You and I can boldly enter God's presence because Christ paved the way for us (Hebrews 10:19-20). The people Moses led out of Egypt don't have that privilege. Their sin still stands between them and God. How can it be moved out of the way? God provides a way through a system of sacrifices. The penalty for sin is death. Therefore, through the sacrifices, an animal's life is offered in place of the life of the worshiper. But not just any animal will do. God has very specific requirements, because ultimately, these sacrificial animals foreshadow what God's own Son will do on the cross.

The second half of Exodus and all of Leviticus are set on the plains surrounding Mount Sinai. After leading Israel through the Red Sea, God brings the people here. Moses goes up on the mountain to receive God's Law. When he comes down, the people stay put while they build the tabernacle and begin worshiping God in the way he requires. Only then will they be ready to head to the Promised Land.

Leviticus 1–7

The book of Leviticus describes five types of sacrifices the people are to offer: burnt offerings, grain offerings, peace offerings, sin offerings, and guilt offerings. Each one is an enacted prayer that outwardly expresses what the worshipers feel in their hearts. When a worshiper offers a sheep or a goat on the altar, he is telling God, "The fate that is about to befall this animal is what I deserve for my sin." The burnt offering expresses a total dedication of oneself to God. The sin and guilt offerings are given to gain forgiveness from God for sins committed unintentionally. The other two offerings, the grain offering and the peace offering, are ways for people to express their gratitude to God.

Leviticus 8–11
Chapter 10 may sound harsh. As you read it, ask yourself, *What else should God have done?* He has just spent months detailing exactly how he must be approached. Now on the first day of worship in the tabernacle, by the newly ordained priests who are to lead the people into God's presence, two of the priests throw all of God's instructions out the window and do whatever they want. The incense they offer probably reflects the ways people worship idols in Egypt. If God simply lets this slide on the very first day, what will the future hold? Compare this passage to the story of Ananias and Sapphira in Acts 5.

Leviticus 12–15
Welcome to the part of the Law that will leave you saying, "I can't believe *that's* in the Bible!" Keep in mind, the people you're reading about live long before the invention of refrigeration or antibiotics or even the most rudimentary medicines. They also don't have running water or flush toilets or many of the basics of hygiene we take for granted. Illness and disease can spread through their population in an instant. Remember this as you read the rules regarding infectious skin diseases and clean and unclean animals. These chapters may not seem practical to you or me today, but to a group of several million living in tents while traveling through the desert three thousand years ago, these commands show how God is concerned about every aspect of life.

Leviticus 16–23

The key verse for this section is Leviticus 19:2: "You must be holy because I, the LORD your God, am holy." The word *holy* simply means to be set apart, to be different. The laws and commands in these chapters give the children of Israel practical instructions as to how they can be different from the people who don't know God. Many of these laws confront wicked practices that are common in the land the Israelites are about to inhabit, including the practice of having sex with a temple prostitute as a way of insuring a bumper wheat crop the next season, or sacrificing children to appease an angry god. The Lord gives the holiness code of Leviticus as a way of protecting the Israelites from these practices that result in death.

Holiness has never been and can never be achieved by human effort. That's why this section begins with instructions for the annual Day of Atonement, the day when the high priest offers a sacrifice for the sins of the people within the Most Holy Place in the tabernacle. He enters the Holy of Holies and sprinkles the blood of the sacrifice on top of the atonement cover that sits on top of the ark of the covenant. As a result, God's wrath for their sins will be turned away. Romans 3:25 uses the same word for "atonement cover" or "mercy seat" to describe Christ. He is the one who took the punishment for our sins and turned away the wrath of God our sins deserved. He is our place of mercy, the ultimate fulfillment of the Day of Atonement, and the One who now makes us holy, setting us apart for God.

Leviticus 24–27

This section of Leviticus includes instructions for six annual festivals the people of Israel are to observe. The festivals are designed to remind them of all God had already done for them as well as to call them to continue to trust in him daily. These six festivals essentially mean that every two months, they will come together for a special time of worship before God. The Lord does this to make sure they won't become so caught up in the day-to-day business of scratching out a living that they will forget why they are alive.

Chapter 25 describes one of the most radical aspects of God's Law, the Year of Jubilee. In the Year of Jubilee, all debts are supposed to be forgiven. In addition, all the land reverts to the families to whom it was originally given, and slaves are set free. The Year of Jubilee guarantees everyone a new start. It levels the playing field and prevents the radical accumulation of wealth at the expense of others. The year also makes permanent slavery impossible in Israel. Keeping the Year of Jubilee demands a great deal of faith, which is also part of God's plan. Every generation is thus reminded that God and God alone is their sole source of provision.

Numbers

The book of Numbers derives its name from the two censuses of Israel recorded in the book. The two act like bookends, one at the beginning and the other at the end. The first census counts the people who walk out of Egypt under Moses' leadership. The second counts the next generation, the people who will actually enter the Promised Land under Moses' lieutenant and successor, Joshua. In between, the book covers the people's forty years of wandering around in the desert. While God doesn't originally intend for the people to spend decades in the wilderness, his plan includes a two-year stay. Most of the time is spent at Mount Sinai, where the people receive the Law, build the tabernacle, and start worshiping the one true God his way.

Numbers 1–7

The first few chapters of Numbers primarily deal with housekeeping issues within the Israelite camp: counting the fighting men, arranging the tribes in the camp, assigning duties, and chronicling the people's offerings. Numbers 5:11-31 may strike you as odd. As you read, keep in mind the ultimate purpose of these instructions: to protect the sanctity of marriage.

Chapter 6 details the Nazirite vow. This vow means a person dedicates himself to God for a set period of time for a specific purpose. Samson will be a Nazirite from birth (Judges 13–16). Samuel, the last judge before the monarchy, and John the Baptist will also be set apart under Nazirite vows. The apostle Paul will take a similar vow for a set amount of time (Acts 21:15-25). Although the word *Nazirite* doesn't appear in Acts 21, you will recognize the parallels with Numbers 6.

Numbers 8–12

The seventy leaders Moses picks in chapter 11 all receive "some of the Spirit that was upon Moses." The Holy Spirit won't take up permanent residence in every believer until the day of Pentecost in Acts 2. In the Old Testament, the Spirit comes upon people to equip them for the tasks God has for them. Once the task is over, or when a person disqualifies himself for the job, the Spirit leaves him. King Saul in 1 Samuel is an example of this. The giving of the Spirit involves imparting special abilities to do a God-given job, rather than imparting a special relationship with God. That's what will make the pouring out of the Spirit on all believers in Acts such a radical change.

Numbers 13–16

Numbers 13 marks a turning point in this part of God's story. The people the Lord rescued from Egypt finally go too far. When faced with the choice of trusting God or wishing they could go back to the good old days in Egypt, they choose the latter. As a result, God declares that none of the generation who saw all these wonders will survive to enter the Promised Land. What should be a short journey with a long detour to Mount Sinai turns into a forty-year death march. Everyone twenty years of age and older is condemned to die in the wilderness, except Joshua and Caleb, the two spies who trusted God. Faced with the prospect of marching around in sandstorms waiting to die, the people do what you would expect them to do: They complain and rebel and suffer as a result.

What causes the Israelites to become so frightened that they lose sight of God? While the giants in the land aren't twenty feet tall, the average Israelite man probably tops out at only a little more than five feet tall. Therefore, the giants they encounter are very tall, very buff warriors, comparable to Goliath. Remember, Shaq or Kevin Garnett may look normal size on television, but if you stood next to one of them, you too would feel like a grasshopper in comparison.

Numbers 17–20

In the midst of God's punishment, he offers hope. Out of the tragedy of a lost generation (lost by their own choice), God raises up a new generation who will experience the fulfillment of all of God's promises. Yet the story isn't as simple as that. You can see the invisible hand of another Enemy in the book of Numbers. Listen closely, and you can see Satan plotting, trying to find some way to kill God's promises in the Sinai Peninsula. Angry armies ride out and attack God's people, but God always prevails. One king resorts to hiring a prophet to put a curse on Israel. God makes sure a blessing comes out instead. Then the Enemy resorts to an old but effective weapon, lust. Will the people be able to survive their basest instincts?

Numbers 20 is another tragic chapter. There, Moses loses his temper with the people. As a consequence, God doesn't allow him to lead the people into the Promised Land. To find out why, read 20:12. If Moses isn't exempt from God's discipline, shouldn't we be even more careful about how we live?

Numbers 21–28

Compare chapter 21 to John 3:14. The bronze serpent shows up again in the Old Testament. Apparently the people are so touched by this episode that they keep the bronze serpent Moses made. With time they forget about how God delivered them, and they make the snake itself into an idol. Several hundred years later, King Hezekiah destroys it as he tries to purge idolatry from the land.

Another character shows up in this section, a prophet named Balaam. His actions seem to be noble in these chapters. After all, he says he won't say anything except that which God tells him to say. However, later we learn he was also behind Moab's seduction of Israel in chapter 25. The idea seems to be, if you can't curse them, trip them up with lust. You'll see his ultimate fate when you read chapter 31.

Numbers 29–36

The tribes of Reuben, Gad, and half of the tribe of Manasseh receive land on the east side of the Jordan River in what is today the country of Jordan. They occupy the lands taken from the Amorites, Ammonites, and Midianites. For the exact location, check the maps in the back of your Bible. Before Moses agrees to give them this land, he makes them pledge to fight with the rest of Israel for the Promised Land. Only then can they enjoy the land of Gilead, another name for the land east of the Jordan River.

The last few chapters aren't the most exciting in the world. You'll read about how the people are going to divide the land and which cities are to be set apart as "cities of refuge" (a place a person who accidentally kills another could flee for safety). Yet this snoozer of a section records something remarkable. These people who spent nearly four decades in the desert start making plans for life in a land none of them has ever seen. They set aside cities they haven't even built as places of refuge, and they divide mountains and valleys among tribes even though no one has yet set foot there. This is either an act of foolishness or arrogance or incredible faith.

Deuteronomy

The book of Deuteronomy is actually one long speech delivered by Moses shortly before his death. Its name comes from two Greek words that mean "the second giving of the Law." And that's exactly what it is. In this speech, Moses gives the Law to a new generation who arose in the wilderness wandering. Most people assume the Old Testament Law is all about performance. The Israelites had to do all this stuff like sacrificing sheep and not doing any work on Sabbaths and not eating pork, or God would whack them upside their heads. As you read through the second giving of the Law, you will find something else entirely. Instead of a relationship based on performance, we find the word *love* popping up time and again. God chose the Israelites to be objects of his love, and he wants them to love him back. Obedience to the Law isn't a way of working their way into God's favor. Instead, it is to be an act of love for God, a lesson the New Testament Pharisees never grasped.

Deuteronomy 1–5

Moses begins his farewell address with a history lesson. He takes the children of Israel back through their wandering in the wilderness, pointing out God's faithfulness in spite of their constant rebellion. Even the Ten Commandments are given as part of the overall story of how God delivered Israel and called them to be his own people. Over and over Moses tells how God provided for them and fought battles on their behalf. He doesn't come out and say it, but you can hear echoing through his words the encouragement, "What God did before, he will do again." More than anything, Moses doesn't want this new generation to repeat their parents' mistake recorded in Numbers 13. He also stresses the unique standing these descendants of

Abraham have in the world. They alone have been chosen from all the nations on earth to enjoy a unique, intimate relationship with the one true God. The Lord of the universe has made a covenant with them to be their God as they are his people. The laws they are about to hear are the terms of that covenant.

Deuteronomy 6–10
Chapter 6 is the heart of the book of Deuteronomy and the heart of the Law. The Law isn't about obeying rules, but about entering into a loving relationship with the God who created them and chose them to be his own. Pay extra close attention to verses 4-8. Jesus later calls this the first and greatest commandment (Matthew 22:37-39), with the second being to love one's neighbor as oneself (Leviticus 19:18). Again, remember the question posed after the first man and woman sinned and died. This chapter shows how God's purpose for creating people in the first place still applies. He wants us to know him, love him, serve him, and worship him. In short, he wants an eternal, intimate relationship with you and me. The five books of the Law show how God sets out to make this happen, with a people, a promise, a land, and a covenant. The rest of the story, the Prophets and the Writings, tells how well the people live up to their part of the bargain.

Deuteronomy 11–16
Do the laws regarding clean and unclean animals still apply? If they do, you and I can't eat pork or catfish. To do so would be an act of disobedience against God. Before you throw away your jumbo breaded tenderloin sandwich, read Mark 7:17-19 and Romans 14:20. Jesus declares all foods to be "clean"; that is, they can be eaten. Peter also learns this lesson in Acts 10. What we eat doesn't make us more or less acceptable to God. What comes out

of our mouths, our words, matters much more than what we put into them. Why then did God give these dietary laws? Remember, these people lived long before Sears started selling refrigerators. God's concern was for their hygiene and long-term health. Even today we know eating undercooked pork can be fatal.

Deuteronomy 17–22

Chapter 17 gives the regulations for a king, even though the people wouldn't ask for a king for another four hundred years. Compare 17:14-20 with the story of the most successful king Israel ever had, Solomon. You'll find a summary of his accomplishments in 1 Kings 10. Based on Deuteronomy 17, how successful was Solomon in God's eyes?

Deuteronomy 21:22-23 has special significance when read in light of the cross. More than a thousand years before the rise of the Roman Empire (which raised crucifixion to an art form) and fourteen hundred years before the birth of Christ, God addressed the way his Son would die. Check out Galatians 3:13. Because of the laws in Deuteronomy regarding hanging someone on a tree, Paul was able to say:

> Christ has rescued us from the curse pronounced by the law. When he was hung on the cross, he took upon himself the curse for our wrongdoing. For it is written in the Scriptures, "Cursed is everyone who is hung upon a tree."

Is this a coincidence? Or did the God who lives outside of time give the Law with an eye toward the cross?

Deuteronomy 23–30

Deuteronomy 26:16-19 shows how the book fits into the larger story of the Old Testament. Think of this book as a contract.

In it, God tells the people everything they need to do in order for him to live in their presence. Verses 16-19 are like the legal language at the bottom of a contract that appears just before the place for your signature. These are more than regulations in a book. The people have to commit themselves to keep their part of the bargain. It isn't that they can somehow buy God's favor by keeping them. Remember how the first man and woman were driven out of God's presence. Now he is going to dwell among a group of people in a tangible way. Obedience is to be a reflection of the people's love and devotion to God.

Deuteronomy 31–34

The Law reflects God's holiness and design for the human race. Sadly, after the first man and woman sinned, the entire human race changed. They were driven away from God's holy presence, and his design was totally corrupted. In this state, no one would be able to keep the Law. As you read chapter 31, you will see how immediately after Moses finishes writing out the Law, God essentially tells him, "No one will do what you just wrote."

So what was the point of God's giving the people a Law they couldn't keep? Read Romans 3:19-20 for the answer. God gave the Law to show everyone the need for his grace. As long as we can cling to the illusion that we are, in the words of Winnie the Pooh, "all right, really," we will never abandon our attempts to justify ourselves. Without the Law, no one would ever come to Christ. Something as radical as God in flesh dying on a cross wouldn't make any sense. Only when we come face-to-face with the Law can we see our absolute need for Jesus. The rest of the story of the Old Testament drives this point home. Remember, the questions of this story are: "Who is God?" and "How can sinful people live in an intimate relationship with a holy God?" How, indeed.

2

The Former Prophets

Joshua, Judges,
First and Second Samuel,
First and Second Kings

AUTHORS

None of these six books names an author. Jewish tradition holds that Joshua wrote the book that bears his name; Samuel wrote Judges; some unknown prophet wrote 1 and 2 Samuel; and Jeremiah wrote 1 and 2 Kings. No one really knows, because the Bible is completely silent on the question. However, figuring out which prophet actually penned these books doesn't affect their role in the Bible or the power of their message. The authority of a biblical book doesn't come from its human author. The ancient Hebrews and early Christians acknowledged these books' authority because they heard the voice of God in them.

WHEN WERE THESE BOOKS WRITTEN?

Joshua was probably written toward the end of the first wave of the conquest of the Promised Land, in the early fourteenth century BC. Judges may have been written in the early days of the kings, around 1000 BC. Since Samuel focuses on the way Israel gained a king and the covenant God made with David, it was probably written shortly after David died in 965 BC. The books of Kings had to be written after the people of Israel were carried off into exile when Babylon destroyed Jerusalem in 586 BC.

WHAT ARE THEY ABOUT?

Together, these six books tell *what happens* to Abraham's descendants from the time they enter the Promised Land (1400 BC) until they are carried away by force (586 BC), a period of about eight hundred years. The writers show how every twist and turn in the story is directly related to how faithful these people were to the one true God and his covenant with them. The Lord chose these people to know him and make him known to the world. He told Moses and Israel what would be required to live in his presence. These books answer the question: Will they do it?

Joshua

Plot: The people conquer Canaan under the leadership of Joshua, Moses' successor. After the initial battles, the land is divided between the twelve tribes. The individual tribes then continue driving out the Canaanites, Hittites, Jebusites, and all the other "ites" who lived in the land God promised to Abraham and his descendants.

Key characters: Joshua, Rahab, Caleb, the Canaanite kings

Turning point in the story: Joshua 11

Judges

Plot: Judges chronicles the days before Israel had a king. You will find a recurring pattern. When times are good, the people forget about the Lord and adopt the gods and practices of the surrounding nations. God then punishes Israel by sending armies to oppress them. Once they become miserable enough, the Israelites cry out to God for deliverance. The Lord then raises up a judge to deliver the people, resulting in a few decades of peace and prosperity. As soon as the good times return, the pattern repeats itself.

Key characters: Deborah, Barak, Gideon, Samson (the latter three are listed in the "Faith Hall of Fame" in Hebrews 11).

Turning point in the story: Judges 2

First and Second Samuel (originally one book)

Plot: Together they tell the story of the last judge, Samuel. The books also record the transition from a theocracy, where God reigns as King of Israel, to a monarchy, where a man sits on a throne. The first king looks like the perfect man for the job, but he lacks integrity and character. God then selects a man after his own heart, David. The books tell how God makes a new covenant with David, a promise that is ultimately fulfilled in Jesus.

Key characters: Hannah, Samuel, Saul, David, Jonathan, Joab, Absalom

Turning points in the story: 1 Samuel 16; 2 Samuel 7

First and Second Kings (also written as one book)

Plot: They pick up where Samuel leaves off. Their story starts off with such promise. David's son Solomon takes over after his father's death. All the blessings God promised in Deuteronomy 28:1-12 come true. The people prosper, their influence spreads across the known world, and the kingdom stretches from the Sinai Desert to the Euphrates River. But it doesn't last. The rest of the books record the steady downward spiral as God's chosen people reject him time after time. Ultimately, all the curses God promised in Deuteronomy come to pass, and the people are removed from the land by force.

Key characters: Solomon, Rehoboam, Jeroboam, Ahab, Jezebel, Elijah, Elisha, Jehu, Hezekiah, Manasseh, Josiah

Turning point in the story: 1 Kings 11

Joshua

The book of Joshua is either the story of God's fulfilling his promises to his chosen people or a cruel tale of genocide carried out in the name of religious fervor. The answer depends on your perspective. Skeptics dismiss the God talk in the book and see it as military history. The armies of Israel surround and destroy cities, wiping out entire populations of ethnic groups in the name of God. Not even women or children are spared. If these events took place today, skeptics maintain, Joshua and his generals would be hauled in front of military tribunals and charged with war crimes. How this book could be included in a holy book is beyond them. It simply gives them one more reason to reject God and the Bible.

The story looks completely different when you see it from God's perspective. The book of Joshua is not about armies and conquest, but about one crucial question: Which god is God? Remember, the Lord chose Abraham's descendants to be the vessel through whom he would reveal himself to the world. When the children of Israel walked out with the best Egypt had to offer packed into their wagons, they knew there was no god like the Lord God. Now God would broadcast this same message to all the nations in and around Canaan. People in the ancient Near East viewed success or failure on the battlefield as a religious issue. They prayed to their gods for deliverance and victory. Many carried their gods right out onto the battlefield with them (see 1 Samuel 4:1-9). Therefore, when God ordered the destruction of the people who lived in Canaan, it wasn't a case of genocide, but "theocide." The one true God would soon wipe out all counterfeits.

The Big Question of Joshua

Couldn't God wipe out all the counterfeit gods without killing so many people? If God is love, and if his plan is for all people to come to know him, how could he just wipe out entire populations like this? And if he did, how can we reconcile this with the picture of the loving and forgiving God we see in the New Testament?

When you compare Joshua to the book of Revelation, you find no contradictions at all. At the end of time, all those who oppose God and his Son will be destroyed. When Jesus returns, he will wipe out all the armies of the world just by speaking a word. Then, everyone who has ever lived will stand before him to be judged. Those who never received Christ as their Savior will be separated from God forever. How could a loving God do such a thing? To simply overlook sin and let everyone into heaven would violate his holiness. By giving his Son to die in our place, God maintains his justice while extending his grace. Since Christ died, God has given the people of the world more than two thousand years and counting to turn to him. What more is he supposed to do?

The same is true in the book of Joshua. When God promised to give the land to Abraham and his descendants, he also told him they would have to wait four generations until "the sin of the Amorites has run its course" (Genesis 15:13-16). Simply put, God gave the people in Canaan another four hundred years to repent and turn to him. Once they demonstrated they would never turn away from their false gods, the one true God took drastic action. It was the same kind of action he took with Noah and the Flood, with Sodom and Gomorrah, and ultimately, with the entire earth at the end of time.

Is this fair? Absolutely. And that's what bothers us. We want mercy, not justice. God gave the nations in Canaan justice after several hundred years of offering them grace. Since they wouldn't turn away from their false gods, whose worship included human sacrifice, the Lord destroyed the gods and the people who worshiped them. If he had allowed the people to continue down their current path, not only would future generations pay the price, other nations would become infected with the same cancer. This act of justice will ultimately turn out to be an act of grace for those not yet born — unless, of course, Israel fails to carry out God's commands.

We need to tread lightly here and be careful not to take these ideas further than God intended. Throughout history, nations have used the name of God to justify all sorts of atrocities against people who stood in their way. We need look no further than our own past to find an example. During the nineteenth century, millions of Native Americans were wiped out and their land taken in the name of Manifest Destiny, or the belief that Americans of Anglo-Saxon descent had a divine mission to expand across the North American continent. Joshua stands apart in that God actually did speak to the leaders of Israel, and this came only after he had revealed himself to the people of Canaan and waited more than four hundred years for them to turn to him. As we see in the New Testament, God ultimately wants his followers to tell the nations about him, not kill them.

Joshua 1–5
Rahab the prostitute shows how God offered his mercy to anyone who would accept it. No one did, except this outcast. She makes another appearance later in the Bible. Check out Matthew 1:5. She is the last woman you would expect to find in Jesus' family tree. But isn't that exactly what God's grace does?

Joshua 6–10

Compare chapter 7 to Leviticus 10. The story of the battles for Ai underscores what was said in the introduction to Joshua. The crucial issue in each battle is God's glory and honor, not the Israelite army's military might. Since every battle is a test of deities, those who carry the name of the Lord can't act like everyone else. They must be set apart. They must be holy.

Joshua 11–14

Joshua 11:23 says Joshua takes control of the entire land. Yet chapter 13 says much of the land remains to be conquered. Do these two statements contradict one another? Not at all. Verse 11:23 means all the power bases in Canaan have been destroyed. Now all Israel has to do is spread out across the land and defeat the smaller cities. God told Moses the battles would play out over a long period of time so that each generation would learn to trust him.

Joshua 15–24

The last ten chapters of Joshua are not the most exciting in the world. As you read them, try to see all of this from the perspective of the characters involved. The division of the land among the tribes is the answer to more than four hundred years of waiting. Walking onto their land for the first time is the single greatest moment any of them has ever experienced. For a better understanding of who settles where, refer to the maps in the back of your Bible. Judah is the largest tribe and settles their territory first. Dan is the last to take possession of their land, and even then they don't settle in the allotment Joshua gives them, but move to the far north of the Promised Land.

Judges

Now the story gets interesting. God has given his people a land to call their own. Will the twelve tribes of Israel break the pattern that goes back to Adam and Eve and obey God? Will they become the true chosen people of God and fulfill his purposes for their existence? Will they become a lighthouse to all the nations, the revelation of the one true God to the entire world? Or will they turn away from God and make a joke of his Law just as their ancestors did while they wandered around in the wilderness?

You can probably guess the answer. As you read, ask yourself, *If I were in God's shoes, what would I do? Would I be as patient with the Israelites as he was, and would I continue to give them additional chances?*

Although the book is called Judges, these people didn't hold court like Judge Judy. Instead, they were military leaders who led armies onto the battlefield against God's enemies. They also represented God to the people, just as Joshua did during his life. None was a ruler in the sense of a national king. During this time the nation was a theocracy, which means God was King. This set the people apart from all the other nations.

Judges 1–5

The first generation after Joshua stays close to the Lord. However, as soon as the people who "had seen all the great things the LORD had done for Israel" die, the next generation forgets about God. The roller-coaster pattern of Judges then emerges. When times are good, the people forget the Lord and turn to idols. When times are bad, they turn back to the God of their ancestors. As soon as the good times return, they go back to their idols. The pattern repeats itself throughout this period of Israel's history.

Judges 6–12
The story of Jephthah in chapter 11 is an example of the Bible reporting the acts of its characters without endorsing them. The vow he makes is not only foolish, it is also unnecessary. Nor did Jephthah need to follow through on his vow. If he'd read the Law, he would have known he could have substituted an animal sacrifice for his daughter. His actions reflect a pagan worldview, where the favor of the gods had to be bought. For some reason, God still uses this guy to deliver his people.

Judges 13–16
Samson is both the classic example of wasted potential and proof that God often uses people in spite of their character, not because of it. He could have been one of the greatest heroes of all the Old Testament, a shining example of what can happen when outstanding physical abilities are merged with the unlimited power of God. Instead, his story lives on as a tragic case of what might have been. Samson can't control his lust, and in the end, it costs him everything. He dies alone, abandoned, suffering under the consequences of a lifetime of bad choices.

Judges 17–21
The last five chapters of Judges don't follow any sort of chronology. The stories give you a picture of what life was like when "the people did whatever seemed right in their own eyes" (Judges 17:6). They describe rampant idolatry, treachery, sexual sin, violence, and civil war. These definitely are not the good old days. The stories are disturbing. The most gruesome episode of

CSI hardly compares to what you'll find here. Israel was supposed to be a land where God ruled as King and people did his will as revealed in the Law. Instead, a few generations after entering the Promised Land, they're building idols, trying to force people to engage in homosexual acts, raping women, chopping up corpses, and destroying entire towns. God punished them earlier for such acts, and he was able to get their attention for a short time. How can he persuade anyone to live for him alone for more than a moment or two?

First and Second Samuel

As the days of the judges come to a close, Israel is a mess. Over a period of more than two hundred years, the people have shown they will not keep their part of the covenant God made with them. On the surface it looks like God's grand plan to reveal himself to the world through one nation has failed. What will he do now?

First and Second Samuel begin to answer the question. These two books, which were originally one, start with the story of the last and greatest of the judges, Samuel. He filled the roles of both judge and priest. Toward the end of his life, the people of Israel come to him with a request. They'd grown tired of judges and an invisible King, even if the King was God. They wanted to be like all the other countries around them and have a human king. Their request angers Samuel and God, for it is in essence a rejection of God as King. Why then would God give them one? Does this mean he's switched to "plan B"? Not at all. Watch how the story unfolds. God shows that he can accomplish his plans in spite of human stubbornness.

1 Samuel 1–6

Once again, Israel's battles come down to contests of deities. However, by dragging the ark of the covenant out on the battlefield, the Israelites show how they've confused God with a good luck charm. What happens next shows how God doesn't need a human army to fight his battles. The story of the ark of the covenant being placed in the temple of the Philistine god Dagon is particularly entertaining. Chapter 6 shows how the Philistines have a better handle on the greatness of the Lord than the Israelites do. By the time the Philistines finally get rid of the ark of the covenant, they're the ones asking, "Who is like the Lord?"

1 Samuel 7–10

Baal is the lord of the Canaanite gods who allegedly appears in thunderstorms. His followers claim he can bring rain and make the fields and crops grow. In a land where it doesn't rain for months at a time, he is popular. Worship of Baal includes both animal and human sacrifice. Ashtoreth, like Asherah (another popular idol), is a fertility goddess. In Canaanite mythology, Ashtoreth is Baal's wife, while Asherah is his mother. The goddess's name means "womb" or "that which comes from the womb." Ashtoreth and Asherah are popular for more than one reason. Their "worship" services include sexual acts with prostitutes, both male and female, dedicated to their shrines.

1 Samuel 11–15

Saul looks like a king. He is exactly what the Israelites wanted when they asked Samuel to give them a king like all the other nations. Although Saul reigns over Israel for forty years, with the story of his regime filling all of 1 Samuel, his kingdom essentially ends in chapter 15. Pay close attention to the reason. Also watch his reaction when confronted with his sin. What must run through his mind when he hears Samuel say, in effect, "God has rejected you and found someone better"? How should he respond to this news?

1 Samuel 16–20

What was the chief difference between Samuel's search for Saul in chapter 9 and for David in chapter 16? One looked like a king, the other didn't. Verse 16:7 is a good one to memorize.

The end of chapters 16 and 17 almost seem to contradict one another. In 16 Saul sends for David the son of Jesse to be a part of his court and play the harp for him. Yet after David kills Goliath in chapter 17, Saul has to ask whose son this is. Contradiction? No. Keep in mind how busy the king's court has to be. David is just one of many servants who comes in and out. Moreover, he is just a boy, and a musician at that. After sending for him, Saul probably doesn't think much about who he is. All of that changes when David kills the nine-foot-tall Goliath. At that point Saul takes notice and makes this kid one of his chief warriors.

1 Samuel 21–25

Saul's downfall is his lack of character. By allowing David to endure hardships as an outcast, God provides a classroom in which his character can be fully developed. Saul disqualifies himself for leadership when he takes it on himself to offer sacrifices, a role only a priest could fill. Expedience means more to Saul than obedience. Yet David refuses to harm Saul in any way, even when it appears God has handed him to David. Why? God had anointed Saul as king. Even though David knows God has chosen him to take over the throne, he will not do so by force. David's course isn't the way politics worked in the ancient Near East. New kings often took power by killing the old king. But David refuses to operate by the conventional wisdom. Obedience and trust in God rule his life. The difference in character between David and Saul becomes more and more apparent with each passing day. In the end everyone knows who should be king, even if more delays lie ahead.

1 Samuel 26–31

Two questions jump out from these chapters. First, does the medium Saul consults actually call up the spirit of Samuel? If the answer is yes, does this mean psychics can actually contact the dead? And if it is no, what "spirit" speaks to Saul through the medium? The second question is this: Would David have fought alongside the Philistines against Israel's army if Achish's advisors hadn't objected to his presence? If yes, how could he later serve as Israel's king? And if no, how could a godly man be so deceptive?

2 Samuel 1–6

Why does Uzzah die when he touches the ark in chapter 6? He reaches out to keep the ark of the covenant, the single most holy item in all of Israel, the resting place of the centerpiece of God's covenant with Israel, from falling off a cart. And how does God repay his thoughtfulness? By killing him on the spot. That seems a little extreme, doesn't it? After all, Uzzah was trying to do the right thing. Why does God kill him?

Go back and read Leviticus 10 and Numbers 4:1-15 for insight into why God treats Uzzah as he does. The ark occupied the central place within the most holy part of the tabernacle. It was *the* place where God met with the high priest, making it the symbol of God's presence among Israel. Therefore, when Uzzah reached out and touched the ark, he not only violated the Law, he in effect reached out and touched a holy God. As we saw in Genesis 3, sin can't come into contact with God and survive. It would have been better for him to let the ark hit the ground, because, in God's eyes, dirt is cleaner than a human being since dirt never rebelled against him. It may be hard to grasp, but in the eyes of God, the touch of dirt or grass or weeds would be less offensive than the touch of a human hand.

2 Samuel 7–12

One of the marks of godly character is how a person responds when confronted with his own sin. King Saul would never admit he had done anything wrong. Chapter 11 records David doing something far worse than anything Saul ever dreamed up. Yet notice the difference when Nathan the prophet comes to him in chapter 12. How different might David's legacy have been if he had refused to listen or repent? For insight into David's heart during this time, read Psalms 38 and 51.

Also, pay close attention to chapter 7. It explains why long genealogies can be found in both Matthew and Luke, each one tracing Jesus' family tree back to David. Why couldn't Jesus have been a descendant of Moses or Aaron or Joshua or Joseph instead? What does the family tree of Jesus have to do with 2 Samuel 7?

2 Samuel 13–18

These six chapters officially qualify David's family for the title "dysfunctional." One son rapes his half sister, while her brother takes his revenge and kills the rapist. The same son then undermines his father's authority, ultimately seizing power through a *coup d'état*. To solidify his hold on the nation (and to insult his father), the rebellious son pitches a tent on top of the palace and sleeps with his father's concubines (mistresses who don't enjoy all the rights and privileges of a wife).

Yet none of this happens by chance. The structure of 2 Samuel makes it clear that all of these acts come as a direct result of David's sin with Bathsheba. Along with the death of the baby born from his adultery, the rebellion and violence within his family are part of God's punishment.

Even though God forgave his sin, David still suffers the consequences. Keep in mind, the events in these six chapters take place over six to ten years, maybe more. Notice how David responds. He never gripes. He never shakes a fist at heaven and complains about God's unfairness. Instead, he accepts his consequences and continues to throw himself on the Lord's mercy. This act, as much as his courage when facing Goliath, shows the uncommon faith of this "man after God's own heart."

2 Samuel 19–24

The story of David's reign ends with a confusing episode. David angers God by taking a census. The sin is so great that the Lord sends a plague that takes seventy thousand lives. What did David do to justify such a strong response from God? After all, the United States takes a census every ten years. Are we displeasing God every time we fill out our census questionnaires?

David's census wasn't like ours. Only men of military age were counted. In effect, this census was really a draft for the army. David wanted to know how large a force he possessed. Yet the land was at peace and would remain at peace for the next forty years. His action was completely unnecessary. It also violated the basic tenet of serving as the leader of God's chosen people. As king, David was to show the people how to live by faith. God and God alone was his source of strength and security. By this point God had already made it clear he could wipe out any enemy without human beings taking to the battlefield. Moreover, Israel's battles showed the greatness and glory of God, not her military. The first king in an eternal dynasty had to know this.

First and Second Kings

The history recorded in 1 and 2 Kings is a story of a dying nation. The heights of David's and Solomon's reigns are soon forgotten. Before you dive in, you should reread Deuteronomy 28–30. First and Second Kings are basically these three chapters from Deuteronomy played out in real time. And that's what sets this story apart. The books of the Bible record more than history. They tell God's true story, for God is the One writing history across the pages of time. Nothing happens by chance. He is the Lord of history. Everything he does, he does in accordance with his plan and goals for human beings. That is why the central characters around whom this story is built are not the kings, but those who spoke for God, the prophets.

As you read these books, you'll come across some confusing names, many of which sound alike. Some of the northern kings have the same names as southern kings, and some serve at the same time. It can be confusing. Also, the story of 1 and 2 Kings switches back and forth between the north and the south. You may have to double back from time to time to keep the plotline straight. Through it all, keep in mind the overall plot of this part of God's story. The nation he handpicked is dying a slow and painful death. The cure is as close as a heartfelt, national turn back to the Lord. Even though brief moments of revival are sprinkled into the story, they don't last. The people through whom God planned to reveal himself to the world fail to live up to their part of his covenant. That failure, not economic or military factors, seals their fate.

1 Kings 1–5

The fact that God chooses Solomon, a son of Bathsheba, to be king—especially given her sin with David—shows once again the power of God's grace. And God doesn't just choose Solomon to be king, he pours out his love on him, renaming him Jedidiah, which means "beloved of the Lord." Shortly after Solomon takes his father's throne, the Lord appears to him and offers to give him anything he wants. Solomon asks for the one thing that lives on to this day, wisdom. His request so pleases the Lord that he also gives him riches and fame and honor. In fact, the entire nation enjoys God's blessings on Solomon.

1 Kings 6–10

Four hundred eighty years after Moses built the tabernacle in the wilderness, Solomon builds a permanent replacement in Jerusalem. The temple far exceeds its predecessor's opulence. Solomon spends seven years and uses 188 tons of gold, 375 tons of silver, 675 tons of bronze, and 3,750 tons of iron constructing it (1 Chronicles 29:7). On the day of its dedication, the Lord repeats his miracle in the wilderness as the glory of the Lord fills the temple. In response, Solomon sacrifices 22,000 oxen and 120,000 sheep. As he offers the sacrifices, he asks God to watch over this place and respond to his people as they pray toward it, even if they are far away. God responds by appearing to Solomon a second time and making him this promise: As long as the people walk with him, he will indeed hear the prayers and accept the sacrifices offered in the temple. But if the people run off after strange gods, the Lord vows to destroy the temple and use it as an object lesson to all the people on earth.

1 Kings 11–16

First Kings 11 is the *Titanic* iceberg of the Old Testament. Although Israel will continue on as an independent nation for almost four hundred years after the events of this chapter, her fate is as certain as that of the *Titanic*. The nation will die. All the blessings God showered upon her will evaporate. He will still keep his promises to his chosen people, yet they are the very promises God would rather not keep, the promise to punish her if she as a nation turns away from him. By the time this phase of the story comes to a close, Israel has lost her land, she has ceased to be a great nation, and her name has become a byword among all the other nations. Ten of her tribes have been lost, in a sense gone forever. The two that survive live as captives, exiles in a foreign land. The temple and all its glory has become a pile of broken stones and ashes, the tons of gold and silver and bronze melted down and carried away by an invading army.

The question, therefore, that screams from the page in 1 Kings 11 is why? Why would Solomon, a man to whom God personally appeared on two different occasions, build altars to the pagan deities of Canaan? Not only that, why would a man with so much wisdom do something so stupid? And why would God still include three books penned by Solomon — Proverbs, Ecclesiastes, and Song of Solomon — in the Bible? Remember, if Solomon could fall, what does that say about the human susceptibility to sin? Paul said it best in 1 Corinthians 10:12: "If you think you are standing strong, be careful, for you, too, may fall into the same sin."

1 Kings 17–22

The bad old days have come with a vengeance to the northern kingdom. Although Omri and his son Ahab have raised Israel to its highest levels economically and militarily, the people have never strayed further from God. Baal worship becomes the national religion as Ahab marries the queen of Baal worshipers, Jezebel. Now the people who are supposed to represent God to the world instead export the worship of the worst of all pagan deities. The disease begins to spread south, as Judah looks to her more prosperous sister to the north and imitates her behavior.

This crisis doesn't take God by surprise. He sends the central character of 1 Kings onto the scene, the prophet Elijah. God uses Elijah to confront the entire nation, forcing them to make a choice. First Kings 18 tells one of the greatest stories in the Old Testament, the showdown between God and Baal on Mount Carmel. Like the battles in Joshua and Judges, the chapter shows how the crucial question God shoves in people's faces is "Who is God?" Yet even after such an awe-inspiring demonstration of God's power, the people waver. They may cry out, "The LORD is God," after seeing fire fall from the sky, but their lives don't change. Why? And how much longer can God's patience hold out?

2 Kings 1–5

When Elijah is about to be taken to heaven (being one of only two people in the Bible who didn't die but were taken directly into God's presence), he asks Elisha what he can do for him (2 Kings 2:9). The footnote to the verse in the NLT gives the best translation of Elisha's answer: "Let me inherit a double share of your spirit." Elijah tells him he's asked for a difficult thing, implying only God can answer such a request. And God does. Elisha's recorded miracles outnumber Elijah's two to one. Even after he dies, God's Spirit continues to work through him. A dead man comes to life again after coming into contact with Elisha's bones (2 Kings 13:21).

2 Kings 6–10

Could an ax head really float as recorded in 2 Kings 6? No and yes. In the natural realm, this act was impossible. Iron doesn't float. However, when God gets involved, anything is possible. One old prophet can capture an entire army without firing a shot, through the power of God (2 Kings 6:8-23). He can drive away an invading army and relieve the worst of all famines instantaneously (2 Kings 6:24–7:11). He can cause a barren woman to have a child and even raise the dead (2 Kings 4). With God, nothing is impossible.

2 Kings 11–15

The story of Athaliah shows how God guarantees his covenants in spite of the efforts of men and women to thwart his work. She is the granddaughter of King Omri of the northern kingdom and is as devoted to Baal as her more famous brother, Ahab. In an attempt to solidify her hold on power, she slaughters everyone who could challenge her reign, putting to death every one of her grandchildren. God told David one of his sons would always sit upon the throne, but if every child of the king were put to death, the royal line would end. As always, God raises up someone to keep his plan intact. The dead king's sister hides one infant son, a baby named Joash, thus preserving the line of succession.

The rapid listing of kings in the northern kingdom in chapter 15 shows how the situation there is unraveling. With each passing king, the kingdom is growing a little weaker, a little smaller. Each of the kings in the north is just like the one before. None serves the Lord. Each one continues worshiping idols. You can feel God's patience wearing thin. How long will he wait for these people to turn back to him?

2 Kings 16–20

Assyria and its capital, Nineveh (located in what is today southern Turkey, western Iran, and northern Iraq), is the superpower
of its day. Its empire stretches out across the ancient Near East.
The Assyrian army has earned a reputation for extreme cruelty.
To keep captives from escaping, they drive huge hooks into the
captives' jaws, then join them all together with ropes or chains.
Think of a bunch of fish on a stringer and you have the idea.
Israel, the stronger of the two kingdoms, is no match. Assyria
slaughters her armies, burns her cities to the ground, and drags
the people north to be swallowed up by the empire. The phrase
"the lost tribes of Israel" refers to the ten tribes who disappear
at this time.

   Then the king of Assyria turns his attention to Judah. When
God wants to stress something's importance, he repeats it. The
Law is given twice. The story of Jesus is retold four times.
And the story of the way God destroyed 185,000 Assyrian
warriors in one night is told three times: here, in Isaiah, and
in 2 Chronicles. Notice how Hezekiah understands that battles
aren't fought with swords, but with prayer, for nothing is
impossible for God. Isaiah the prophet makes his first appearance here. He is the same Isaiah who wrote the book of the
Bible that bears his name.

2 Kings 21–25

After David, Hezekiah is one of the two best kings Judah ever
had. His son is the worst. In fact, Hezekiah's son Manasseh is
so bad God's patience finally runs out. In his fifty-five years as
king, Manasseh undoes all the good his father accomplished.
He brings in all the worst the northern kingdom of Israel ever
did. It isn't just the king who is at fault. If the people really buy

into Hezekiah's reforms, why don't they rise up in revolt and refuse to allow Manasseh to plant idols in the temple court?

Manasseh is followed by the other shining example of godliness among the kings, Josiah. He ushers in the last great revival in Israel's history. But once again, the effects are short-lived. His son goes right back to the pagan practices of all the worst kings. Of course, it's too late. The death spiral finally ends. God sends the Babylonians to destroy Judah and tear down the temple in 586 BC. The upper classes are carried off into exile. All the glory of David's and Solomon's days now seems like a fairy tale. The people who were to be a light to the nations are now disgraced. The light is out.

3

The Latter Prophets

Isaiah, Jeremiah, Ezekiel,
Hosea, Joel, Amos, Obadiah,
Jonah, Micah, Nahum,
Habakkuk, Zephaniah,
Haggai, Zechariah, Malachi

AUTHORS
Each book bears the name of its author.

WHEN WERE THESE BOOKS WRITTEN?
Isaiah prophesied before and after the fall of the northern kingdom (roughly 740–690 BC), Jeremiah during the decline and
fall of the southern kingdom (about 646–586 BC), and Ezekiel
during the Jews' exile that immediately followed (about 593–
571 BC). The twelve minor prophets wrote around 760 BC
(Amos) to 450 BC (Malachi).

WHAT ARE THEY ABOUT?
Looking back over the portion of the Old Testament we just
read, we're left with questions. We wonder why God would

allow things to turn out the way they did. Why would he let his chosen people be overrun by an army who worshiped the sun, the moon, and the stars? Why would he allow the temple Solomon spent seven years building to be torn apart by soldiers looking to nab some treasure? Why would he see fit to have Jerusalem, the place whose name means "City of Peace," turned into a bloody battlefield while the civilian population suffered as casualties of war? Why did the story that started out with such hope when Joshua led the people of Israel across the Jordan River end so horribly as Nebuchadnezzar dragged the Jews to Babylon as slaves?

WHY?

The question isn't why God would *allow* these things to happen. After reading Joshua through 2 Kings, we come away knowing God *caused* events to occur as they did. In fact, he warned his people that this was how things would turn out. The book of Deuteronomy is filled with promises of what God would do if the people strayed from him. They strayed, and he made good on his word. Yet in spite of his judgment, God made sure some of his people survived. Their survival would stand as a testimony to the entire world that the destruction of the Jewish nation was more than a coincidence or the unfortunate convergence of a shrinking power suffering at the hand of a rising tyrant. No, God wanted all people for all time to know he caused this. But why?

The fifteen books of the Bible known as the Latter Prophets set out to answer that question. As Paul Harvey would say, we are now about to hear the rest of the story. We just read what happened to Israel. Now we will hear God's commentary on the same events. He will explain to us in chilling detail why he did what he did. Don't expect some cold reporting of facts. These books bring you face-to-face with God's passion. He speaks not as a disinterested observer but as a scorned lover and a brokenhearted father. These books show us the lengths to which God will go to pull his people back to himself.

Some people don't like the way God comes across in the Prophets. They say he sounds too angry, too vengeful, too unloving. And he *is* angry. Very angry. Of course, you might be angry too if the woman you loved and pledged your heart to ran off and became a prostitute as a way of spiting you. And you might be ready to dish out a little justice to those who abused widows and orphans and used the courts as a pretense to enable the rich to steal from the poor. Not long ago the national news told the story of a woman who threw her two infant sons off a bridge and into the Mississippi River below. Those who heard the story were outraged. Imagine how God felt as he watched people who were supposed to love him throw their infant children into a fire as sacrifices to fertility gods.

The picture of God painted by the prophets is anything but unloving. God's love prompts him to do something about the horrific moral condition of his chosen people. He can't sit idly by and watch them destroy themselves, because he loves them too much. So he sends his prophets to warn the people and call them back to himself. No matter what Israel and Judah go through, God makes sure someone is there to speak for him. And the message is always the same: Come back to me; come back to the One who loves you with a love far greater than anything you can comprehend. If you come back, I will sweep you up in my arms and forgive you and pour out my love on you. But if you don't, judgment will come upon you. These themes of sin, punishment, and restoration run through every one of the prophets. God says his people have sinned and will soon be punished, but he longs to restore them to fellowship with him.

Most of the latter prophets wrote in Hebrew poetry. Instead of using rhyme, they repeated ideas from one line to the next. Some people find this confusing. After all, if this is part of the story, why isn't it written as story? Yet these books form an integral part of the overall story of God. In them God speaks. He shows us his perspective on the events we read about in the Former Prophets, and he tells us what he plans to do about it. The books also give us the first indication that more of the story remains to be written. If it weren't for the Latter Prophets, we wouldn't expect the next part of God's story, the New Testament. After reading the Prophets, we wouldn't expect anything less.

Isaiah

Plot: Isaiah's ministry spans the reigns of Kings Uzziah, Jotham, Ahaz, and Hezekiah. He arrives on the scene to tell the southern kingdom of Judah exactly what the Lord is doing in destroying the northern kingdom. He also calls the people who remain to turn from their sin to God.

Key characters: God, Isaiah, Hezekiah, Assyria, Babylon

Turning point in the story: Isaiah 53

Jeremiah

Plot: Like Isaiah, Jeremiah tells the people exactly what the Lord is doing. He makes sure they don't think these are random events. As God's spokesman, he tells the people they've offended a holy Lord and will now pay the price.

Jeremiah is known as the weeping prophet, for he shared God's great sorrow for his people.

Key characters: God, Jeremiah, Baruch, Judah's kings, Babylon

Turning point in the story: Jeremiah 31:31-40

Ezekiel

Plot: Ezekiel doesn't just speak to the Jewish exiles in Babylon, he lives through their experience. Unlike the northern kingdom, the exiles in Babylon will have an opportunity, in a few decades, to return to the Promised Land. Therefore, God sends his spokesman to get them ready. Once again, the Lord wants the people to know he is responsible for what has happened to them, and he wants them to be clear about the reason why he did what he did. Ezekiel offers them real hope in spite of their captivity and suffering. All they have to do is turn back to the Lord.

Key characters: God, Ezekiel

Turning points in the story: Ezekiel 33:21-33; 37

The Minor Prophets

Plot: The three themes of sin, punishment, and restoration flow through all twelve. We also get a unique look at God's character. He shows himself to be much more willing to forgive than we are to tell other people about him.

Key characters: The authors whose names are on the twelve books

Turning point in the story: Malachi 4. The last promise in the last book chronologically in the Old Testament points to the coming of "Elijah" (John the Baptist) to pave the way for the Messiah. The last promise of the Old Testament is the first promise fulfilled in the New Testament.

Isaiah

Isaiah served as a prophet in Jerusalem for more than fifty years, from the reign of King Uzziah until the days of Manasseh. When he first started preaching, the southern kingdom of Judah was in the middle of a cultural and economic renaissance. By the time he died, Judah was little more than a shell of what it had once been, and the northern kingdom was no more. Isaiah watched the downward spiral and called the people back to God. This moment of history is one of the key turning points in the story of Abraham's descendants. The loss of the northern kingdom and the permanent disappearance of part of the tribes of Israel was one of the worst chapters in Israel's history. That is why God placed Isaiah in the midst of it all. He was the Lord's light in the darkness. Jewish tradition says Manasseh, the worst of all the southern kingdom's kings, had Isaiah stuffed into a hollow log and sawn in half.

Isaiah 1–4

Of all the prophets, Isaiah was the most eloquent, as the first chapter shows. Here the prophet makes you feel God's broken heart and his anger over his people's sin. Yet amid promises of judgment, the Lord calls his people back to himself. He vows to restore them to intimate fellowship with him if they turn from their sin. Isaiah also holds out hope for greater days when Israel's glory will be restored. This final promise won't be fulfilled until Christ returns. The rest of the book follows the same pattern. This chapter is especially powerful when you read it immediately after reading through 1 and 2 Kings.

Isaiah 5–8

After you read chapter 5, turn to Mark 12:1-12. Jesus retells
the story of the vineyard with a twist. He indicts the Pharisees
as the ones responsible for the vineyard's condition. No wonder
they become so angry when they hear this story. Isaiah uses
this story to explain why God will soon destroy Judah. The
Pharisees hear Jesus tell them they are about to suffer the same
fate. To their ears, Jesus' words mean they are as bad as the
people to whom Isaiah wrote. That isn't exactly a compliment.

The book of Isaiah isn't written chronologically. Chapter 6
tells how God called him to become a prophet. In Hebrew (the
language in which the Old Testament was written), the way to
emphasize something is to repeat it. Repeating something three
times places the ultimate emphasis on it (think big, bigger,
biggest). Remember this as you hear the angels cry out, "Holy,
holy, holy is the Lord God Almighty." Before Isaiah becomes
a prophet, the Lord shows him his awesome holiness. Isaiah
never gets over the image. He emphasizes the Lord's holiness
throughout the book.

Isaiah 9–12

Chapter 9 focuses on the coming Messiah and the hope he will
bring. Again, notice how the call to repent, warnings of judgment, and the future hope God gives are all woven together.
You can't separate one from another. Jesus will follow this same
pattern as he speaks. He will call people to a new relationship
with him and pronounce judgment on those who reject him.
His message will parallel that of the prophets.

Chapter 11 describes the coming Messiah. The Savior will
be a direct descendant of King David. Most of the promises
in the chapter have yet to be fulfilled. They describe the time

when Jesus will reign over the earth. Only when the Prince of Peace sits on his throne will there be real peace on earth. Chapter 12 then sounds a lot like the Great Commission. As we experience the hope Christ gives, we too will want to "make known his praise around the world" (12:5).

Isaiah 13–17

Chapter 14 is often interpreted to be an account of the fall of Satan. According to this view, Isaiah's description of the fall of the king of Babylon is actually a description of Satan being kicked out of heaven. The King James Version follows the Latin Vulgate and uses the name Lucifer (which means "light bearer") in place of the words "shining star" (14:12). Those who hold to this view go into great detail about how Satan's pride and desire to exalt himself above God led to his ouster. However, nothing in this text indicates Isaiah is talking about anyone other than the king of Babylon. The name Isaiah uses for the king ("shining star, son of the morning" in the New Living Translation or "morning star" in the New International Version) actually mocks the king. Isaiah compares him to a star that shines briefly in the morning but soon fades away. That, says the prophet, is exactly what will happen to the king of Babylon. He and everything he does will soon fade away and be forgotten.

Isaiah 18–21

Chapter 20 is definitely a "don't try this at home" chapter. God tells Isaiah to walk around barefoot and naked for three years as a visual sermon of the troubles God will bring upon Egypt and Ethiopia. Even though the command sounds strange, Isaiah does it. Think about this for a moment. Put yourself in his place. Isaiah was a real man who lived in the real world. What must have run through his mind during these three years? And what do you think his friends and family thought?

Isaiah 22–25

Some, not all, of Isaiah's prophecies speak of a time that still hasn't taken place. Chapter 24 is one of those passages. While the other prophecies in chapters 13–23 speak of what will happen when God judges the northern and southern kingdoms, chapter 24 looks ahead to the day when the Lord will judge the entire earth. Compare it to Revelation 19. A day is coming when God, the righteous judge, will come to earth and destroy it. He will lay waste its rulers and wipe out everything people of the world cling to. Yet the day will be glorious, for the Lord will also establish his throne on Mount Zion. He will rule gloriously, and the light of his glory will drown out the sun and the moon. Chapter 25 describes the marvelous aftermath of his judgment.

Obviously, this prophecy has not yet been fulfilled. The Bible doesn't go into great detail about the events that will lead up to this day, at least not enough detail for us to predict when it will happen. And that is by design. The point of promises like Isaiah 24 is not to send us off searching for signs of the times. Instead, God lays this hope before us to encourage us to continue to serve and trust in him.

Isaiah 26–30

Why would God vow to do all the horrible things Isaiah prophesies? Verse 30:18 gives the answer: "But the LORD still waits for you to come to him so he can show you his love and compassion." God isn't getting even with the people by sending destruction. Nor does he find any pleasure in wiping out wicked people. In fact, when you look at what God does to Israel and Judah, the only real question is what took him so long? More than five hundred years pass between the days of the judges and Isaiah's prophecies. Even then, God waits another 120 years before Babylon carries Judah into exile. Put yourself in God's place. What would you do? And would you wait so long to act?

One note: Verses 30:19-22 speak of how the Jews will finally get rid of their idols. After their Babylonian captivity, the Jews will never again have a problem with idolatry. It takes over a millennium, from Rachel's stealing her father's idols to King Manasseh's building Asherah poles in the temple, but they finally get it. The Lord alone is God, and you will worship only him. After spending seventy years in exile, they finally hear the message loud and clear.

Isaiah 31–35

The constant refrain of judgment, judgment, judgment can become tedious to read. However, notice how these chapters place equal emphasis on the hope God gives. Chapter 35 describes why he will one day judge his people. His act of judgment on sin merely paves the way for God's people to finally become what he has always wanted them to be. Songs of mourning will give way to joy and gladness. Remember, God doesn't find pleasure in destroying wicked people. But, when they consistently flip the bird toward heaven and tell God to drop dead, what choice does God have but to finally deal with them?

Isaiah 36–40

Chapter 40 marks a turning point in Isaiah's prophecies. The tone changes as God speaks more like a tender father in chapter 40. The

chapter declares God's greatness and his eagerness to come to
the aid of those who fear him. Judah's rampant idolatry, especially during the reign of Hezekiah's son Manasseh, wears righteous people out. Their hearts break every time they walk
outside. Moreover, wicked people oppress those who love God.
The ungodly use their positions of power to take what they
want by force. Verses 40:27-31 describe the exhaustion of the
righteous and God's provision for them. Verse 31 is perhaps the
most memorized passage in all of Isaiah.

Isaiah 41–45

Isaiah 42:1-4 is the first of four "servant songs." Each of the
songs builds on the others. Together they paint a picture of
the coming Messiah. Yet the picture isn't of a conquering king.
Instead, the later songs show how the Servant will suffer. The
first song tells us he will come to bring justice to all who have
been wronged. He's going to make things right in this world.
The mission of the Servant of the Lord is to spread truth and
righteousness throughout the entire earth. The message sounds
great to the oppressed, but it doesn't sound too good to the
oppressors. No wonder they kill the Servant when he shows up
seven hundred years later.

One of the themes of the second half of Isaiah is the foolishness of idol worship. Chapter 44 is one of the best examples of
this. The chapter takes a humorous, sarcastic tone as it tells of
a man who chops down a tree. He takes part of the tree and
burns it to heat his house. He cooks his bread over another part
of it. And the rest he takes and makes into an idol to worship.
"Yet he cannot bring himself to ask, 'Is this thing, this idol that
I'm holding in my hand, a lie?'" That's God's message to the
world. *All your gods are lies. Worshiping them is foolish because*

they are nothing. Stop wasting your time and come worship me, the one true God who made you.

Isaiah 46–50

Chapter 49 is especially important to those of us who were not born Jews. Verses 1-7 are the second servant song. They make it clear that the coming Servant of the Lord is not just for the Jews alone. He comes as a light to the Gentiles and a way of salvation for the entire earth. The Servant of the Lord would fulfill God's plan to reveal himself to the world. Pay particular attention to verse 4. The Servant describes his work as a failure. He looks at what he has done and sees little if anything is permanent. This verse describes the way Jesus' work appeared at the end of his life. When he died, everyone abandoned him. Even after he ascended into heaven, his followers numbered only 120. Who would have guessed a life that seemed to produce so few results would change the course of human history and touch the entire world?

The third servant song appears in 50:4-11. This is the first of the four that shows the suffering that awaits the Servant of the Lord. He will be rejected, beaten, and spit upon. This song foreshadows Jesus' trial and his walk through the streets of Jerusalem with the cross strapped to his back. Yet the song also sets the stakes. The Servant must be obeyed. God pronounces woe upon those who go their own way and ignore his Servant.

Isaiah 51–56

Isaiah 52:13–53:12 stands out as one of the greatest passages in the entire Bible. This is the passage Jesus referred to when he said, "It was written long ago that the Messiah must suffer and die and rise again on the third day" (Luke 24:46). Peter explains Jesus' ministry through this passage (1 Peter 2:21-25). You can hear this fourth servant song in Paul's words to the Philippians: "Your attitude should be the same that Christ Jesus had . . ." (Philippians 2:5-11). Reading this song, you feel as though you are standing at the foot of the cross. Yet this isn't the only servant song that transports us to the cross. The third song, 50:4-11, also paints a picture of the Servant of the Lord as a suffering, rejected Servant.

The Jews do not apply the servant songs to Jesus. They see in them the suffering of the entire Jewish nation. They are the collective "servant" of the Lord. The Messiah won't suffer, he will correct all suffering. In their hearts they believe he will come as a conquering king, never as a suffering servant. Prior to Jesus' coming to earth, none of the religious experts ever imagined the Messiah would come twice, the first time to save the world from sin, and the second to take his throne on the earth.

The final servant song is followed by a promise of future glory for Jerusalem and an invitation for everyone to turn from sin to God. The New Testament repeats this pattern—the story of Jesus' death, burial, and resurrection is followed by the command to take the gospel to the entire world. The Servant of the Lord has died to reconcile the world to God. Now is the time to take that message of God's love to everyone who will listen. As chapter 56 says, "My blessings are for the Gentiles, too." Christ died for the entire world. In him the plan God began with Abraham reaches its climax.

Isaiah 57–61

When Jesus makes his first public speech, he reads chapter 61: "The Spirit of the Lord is upon me, because he has appointed me to preach Good News to the poor" (Luke 4:18). After reading this chapter, he sits down and tells the crowd, "This Scripture has come true today before your very eyes!" (Luke 4:21). Jesus understands his mission in light of what his Father has already revealed through Isaiah. The people automatically make the connection not only with chapter 61, but with all the other promises regarding the Messiah found in Isaiah. That's why they become angry and drive him away. They can't accept a carpenter's son from Galilee as the Messiah.

Isaiah 62–66

Verse 65:1 is particularly important for you and me and every other Gentile ever born. The people who found the Lord even though they weren't looking for him are we who were not born as part of the Jewish nation. The verses also tell us about the way God works. He seeks us. We do not first seek him. And he isn't far away. His message is simple: "I am here!" And his arms are open.

Isaiah closes with the first detailed description of the new heavens and new earth God will establish after the Final Judgment. Revelation goes into even more detail, but Isaiah makes it clear that a time is coming when all the aftereffects of Adam and Eve's sin will be removed once and for all. God guarantees his promise with these simple words: "I, the LORD, have spoken!" (66:2).

Jeremiah

God speaks through Jeremiah as a wounded lover. He stands before his bride, his chosen people, with a broken heart. The one he chose and called his own hasn't just strayed. She's become a spiritual prostitute, giving herself without shame to one lover after another. After waiting and waiting and waiting and waiting for her to come back to him, God has finally had enough. Yet even as he pronounces her sentence, you can hear his passionate calls for his bride to come home. His arms are open wide. He longs to forgive her and hold her once again. But even as the walls of Jerusalem crumble around her, she refuses his appeals.

You can hear God's passion because Jeremiah shares it. He, more than any other spokesman for God, mourns and weeps over those who will soon taste the full impact of God's judgment. Because of this, the book has a more personal feel than perhaps any other in the Bible. As you read, you feel as though you are looking directly into Jeremiah's soul. At times you will feel compelled to look away. Jeremiah is open and honest, both with his readers and with God. Several times he looks toward heaven and screams out, "Why are you doing this to me?" God's responses aren't what you would expect. These conversations alone make this book well worth the time you will spend reading it.

Jeremiah 1–4

God calls Jeremiah, the son of Hilkiah, one of the priests from Anathoth, to be his prophet during the fall of Jerusalem and the destruction of the southern kingdom of Judah (586 BC). Jeremiah's ministry begins in the middle of the reign of Josiah and continues for forty years. During this time, most of the Jews believe God will always protect them regardless of the way they live. After God rescued Jerusalem from the Assyrians during the reign of Hezekiah, most people came to believe Jerusalem would never fall, because God wouldn't abandon his temple. This belief, combined with the messages of peace and safety from false prophets, makes Jeremiah look like a freak. No one listens to him, even though God himself plants his words inside Jeremiah. Faithfulness and divine anointing don't mean success in this world, but why would we think they would?

Jeremiah 5–8

Compare 5:1 with Genesis 18:16-33. There, Abraham begged God to spare Sodom and Gomorrah if ten righteous people could be found. They couldn't. Only Lot and his family survived, and, if you remember the story, they weren't exactly stellar examples of faith in action. Now God is the one who initiates the type of conversation he had with Abraham in Genesis. Instead of sparing the city for the sake of ten righteous people, God says he will spare Jerusalem if even one can be found.

Verses 5:30-31 are chilling. These verses, along with 6:10-17 and 8:4-7, make it clear the people don't lack information about God. Nor do they lack warning of what may happen if they keep going down the road they are traveling. They know what they're doing, and they don't care. Most live without a thought as to what God may think. If that attitude sounds familiar, it should. People haven't changed. And they never will apart from God's grace.

Jeremiah 9–12

Chapter 12 is the first of Jeremiah's complaints against God. Read it slowly, especially God's reply. When we follow God by faith and fulfill his plan with our lives, it doesn't mean we become robots with plastic smiles on our faces. Jeremiah is worn out. He keeps preaching, but no one listens. In fact, the very people he condemns prosper. Based on outward results, the bad guys appear to be winning. Fatigue finally overwhelms him, along with the thought that he is wasting his life. "How long, God," he finally asks, "how much longer?"

Jeremiah 13–16
Verses 15:10-21 contain Jeremiah's second complaint to God. The Lord's response differs from his earlier one, when he told Jeremiah to buck up, because things were going to get much worse quickly. Here God encourages his prophet and assures him he will protect him. Even though the entire nation turns against him, God will make Jeremiah as strong as a fortified wall. No one will defeat him, for God will protect and deliver him. As you read in future chapters of all Jeremiah suffered, does it sound like God is protecting him?

Jeremiah 17–20
Many of the pagan shrines are located in the valley of Hinnom (chapter 19), including one to the fire god Molech. The Molech shrine consists of a bronze statue with its arms held out. The statue's belly is open. Molech's priests build a fire inside the statue, then children are tossed into its red-hot arms as sacrifices. After the people return from Babylon and rebuild Jerusalem, the valley of Hinnom becomes the city dump. Garbage burns constantly or rots away as it is eaten by maggots. By the time of Jesus, "the valley of Hinnom" will be "gehenna." Jesus will use it as an example of the horrors of hell (Mark 9:47-48).

As Jeremiah's confrontations become more pointed, the nation's leaders become more and more angry. Verses 18:18-23 record the first of many attacks Jeremiah withstands. This one is tame compared with what comes later in the book. Yet nothing the people do can shut him up. He refuses to be silent; chapter 20 tells us why.

If you've never been angry with God because obeying him ruined your life, you won't be able to relate to 20:7-18. The words Jeremiah uses in 20:7 are also used to describe a woman being overpowered and raped. This chapter almost sounds like the book of Job. You can hear Jeremiah's agony. He wants to stop talking about the Lord, he wants to stop spreading this message of doom and gloom, but he can't. God forces the words out of him. Passages like this give us a complete picture of what it means to live by faith.

Jeremiah 21–24

As you read chapter 24, think about why God allowed Jacob's family to move to Egypt back in Genesis. Although they became slaves, the four hundred years they spent in Egypt were crucial to the overall story. Without the isolation living in Goshen provided, Jacob's seventy descendants would never have become a nation. Instead, they would have melted into the people of Canaan through intermarriage. Jeremiah 24 shows how God has something similar planned for the people carried off as exiles to Babylon. Some captives have already been taken, including the prophet Daniel (with a group exiled in 605 BC) and the prophet Ezekiel (with a group taken in 597 BC). These captives aren't the worst of the worst. Instead, God sees hope in many of them. Just as they were shaped by their time in Egypt before God gave them the Promised Land the first time, the Jews will be forever changed by their time in exile. What appears to be a horrible experience will in fact turn out to be an expression of God's grace.

Jeremiah 25–28
Chapters 26–28 give us a glimpse of Jeremiah's day-to-day life. In chapter 26, the leaders almost succeed in killing him. If not for divine intervention in the form of wise words from some of the elders, Jeremiah would have met the same fate almost every other prophet suffered. By the way, the story about the prophet who was hunted down and killed in 26:20-23 is pretty typical of the life of most prophets. People not only rejected their messages, they killed them to shut them up. Why then should it surprise us to find the world is less than thrilled to have us tell them about the one true God?

In chapters 27–28, we find God telling Jeremiah to perform another visual sermon. He makes himself a wooden yoke like those used with oxen and walks around with it over his shoulders. By doing so he tells the people to submit to the Babylonians and not fight going into exile. The prophets who specialize in happy messages don't like this. Chapter 28 tells how one confronts Jeremiah. Most people prefer happy messages. Popularity doesn't make one right.

Jeremiah 29–32
Chapter 31 records the heart of Jeremiah's message. In fact, this may be the most important chapter in the Old Testament. In it, God promises to make a new covenant with his people. As you read about the new covenant in 31:31-37, you are reading one of the foundational stones upon which the New

Testament is built. Christ will come to establish this new covenant, not only with the Jews, but with non-Jews as well. No longer will God's Word be written on tablets of stone. Now he writes his Word in our hearts. This is the first allusion to the promise that God will one day place his Spirit within the heart of every believer.

Jeremiah 33–36

Chapter 36 shows how the people treat Jeremiah's messages. By this point in his ministry, most people have a healthy fear of him. They don't like what he has to say, but they know his predictions come true. Jeremiah writes all his messages onto a scroll and has his servant, Baruch, read it before the people at the temple. The words scare them to death. The elders then send Baruch to the king to read the messages to him. Pay close attention to the king's response. Try to picture him in your mind as he cuts up each page and throws the pieces in the fire. My favorite line in this entire episode is verse 32. Jeremiah writes everything out again on another scroll, only this time, he adds much more!

Jeremiah 37–40

Chapters 39–40 tell us a lot about Jeremiah's character and passion. By this point, he has been preaching without results for nearly forty years. The Babylonians show him honor and respect, as well they should, because he has told the Jews to give up and stop fighting a war they could never win. He could go to Babylon with the exiles and live in comfort and security. Jeremiah chooses instead to stay in Judah with the outcasts. Why? That's where God wants him, but that's also where his heart tells him to stay.

Jeremiah 41–44

After Nebuchadnezzar's army destroys Jerusalem (just as Jeremiah had predicted), you would think the people left behind would be more inclined to heed his advice. But of course, they aren't. These chapters record how some of those left in the land try to escape to Egypt. They drag Jeremiah along with them as a captive. This allows Jeremiah to extend his ministry to the Jews who live in Egypt already, Jews who have worshiped Egyptian gods for generations. Notice the role men and women each play in the worship of these idols in chapter 44.

Jeremiah 45–48

Chapters 46–48 echo parts of Isaiah. Jeremiah speaks to the nations surrounding Israel and Judah. This shows, once again, that God's plan includes the whole world. Although he chose the Jews as the people through whom he would make himself known, God never meant to imply he didn't love the rest of the world. Notice how the themes of sin, punishment, and restoration are woven within these chapters.

The nations addressed surround Judah and Israel geographically. Philistia lies to the west next to the Mediterranean Sea on the plains of Sharon. The word *Palestine* comes from the words *Philistia* and *Philistines*. Moab is east of the Dead Sea; Ammon is east of the Jordan River (in modern-day Jordan); Edom is south and east; Kedar and Hazor are north and east of Moab. Elam lies north of the Persian Gulf (in what are Kuwait and southern Iraq today). Damascus refers to the same site as modern Damascus, then and now the capital of Syria.

Jeremiah 49–52

Chapter 52 retells the story of the fall of Jerusalem, with new and more graphic details. Jeremiah closes with this story to make it very clear that the fate that befell the Jewish people didn't happen by chance. God orchestrated these events. Jerusalem fell, and the people were exiled, because they prostituted themselves to other gods. Not only did Jerusalem fall, but the temple was completely destroyed. All the sacred objects were cut up or melted down. This new captivity will last seventy years, no less, in spite of the happy messages of false prophets. But God doesn't abandon his people there. He sends Ezekiel, his prophet, as spokesman, to speak to them in their exile.

Ezekiel

Ezekiel's audience had already lost everything, as he himself had. They had been carried off to Babylon by Nebuchadnezzar in his first waves of attacks against Judah. Ezekiel himself was taken captive in 597 BC (ten years before Jerusalem's final destruction) and resettled along the Kebar River in what is today Iraq. But most of the exiles expected their stay to be short. They assumed they would be allowed to return home in a matter of months, or at the most a year or two. In their eyes, this unpleasant turn of events was nothing more than the normal ebb and flow of power that marked international politics in the ancient Near East.

Ezekiel walked onto the scene to announce that the Jews' troubles had only just begun. He told them to stop dreaming of going home, for they would be stuck in Babylon until the full force of God's wrath had been poured out. And he also made it very clear that this turn of events was no coincidence. Instead, it was a direct act of God. The exiles and their forefathers had offended God for generations. Now they were being judged, and their punishment was only getting started.

By this point in reading the Latter Prophets, you may be tired of reading messages of doom and gloom. God sounds so angry, so hurt, so vengeful. Yet if you listen closely, you can hear God's love overflow through Ezekiel and the other prophets. Which would be the more loving thing for God to do: to allow his people to sink so far into idolatry that they completely forget who he is, or to rescue them from their sin? God punished the Jews for the same reason a parent punishes a child who runs into the street. Correction and discipline are never fun, yet our lives depend on them. Not only did the Jews' life as a nation depend on God acting decisively, our spiritual life did as well.

Ezekiel 1–5

The four living creatures in Ezekiel 1 can also be found in Revelation 4. The creatures are a type of angel whom God entrusts with standing guard. In Ezekiel they guard God's throne and glory. The wheel within a wheel represents the Spirit of God, which is able to move wherever God decides to go. The eyes covering the wheels represent God's omniscience. Nothing escapes his notice. He sees everything and goes everywhere. The creatures and the Spirit appear to Ezekiel as God calls him to be his prophet to the people in exile in Babylon.

Ezekiel 6–10

God carries Ezekiel in a vision from the Kebar River to the temple. There, he watches as the Spirit of God arises and departs. In that moment the temple becomes just another building. Once the Holy God leaves that place, it ceases to be holy. A few years after his vision, the Babylonians will tear the temple down and melt down all the sacred objects. Although the Bible doesn't give any details, it is likely the ark of the covenant is stripped of its gold and the remaining wooden box destroyed. Through this vision, Ezekiel is able to answer the biggest "why" of all: Why would God allow his house to be destroyed? Later, God gives Ezekiel a vision of a new temple, a permanent place where God will dwell among his people. As always, judgment is followed by the hope of restoration.

Ezekiel 11–16

Chapter 16 retells the Jews' history in a nutshell. The chapter echoes the emotional volume of Jeremiah. The Message's translation of this chapter is especially powerful. The point of this chapter is for you, the reader, to put yourself in God's shoes.

If this happened to you, what would you do? What thoughts would run through your head? What emotions would hit you? This chapter goes beyond explaining why God did what he did to Israel and Judah. It should cause us to pause and wonder what idols we serve in our hearts. We may not bow down before an idol made of stone, but if we dedicate our lives to chasing after material possessions, are we any different from the people Ezekiel called to come back to the Lord? God chose us and chased us down with his grace. How do we respond to his kindness on a daily basis? Have we sold our souls in pursuit of poor substitutes for the one true God?

Ezekiel 17–22

Chapter 18 reveals God's plan in thrusting the Jews into the furnace of judgment. "Do you think," he asks, "that I like to see wicked people die?" (verse 23). Judging from the amount of death and destruction we see in the prophetic books, we might be tempted to answer yes. But God answers his question for us: "Of course not! I only want them to turn from their wicked ways and live" (18:23). The severity of punishment dished out doesn't reveal a vindictive God. Instead, it shows how strong a hold sin has on the human heart. Even after God goes to such extreme measures, people still cling to their idols instead of turning to him. What we often think of as cruelty from God is in fact his mercy. The prophets show he will go to any lengths necessary to turn hearts to him. He does this because he loves us. Where would you be if he didn't?

Ezekiel 23–28

As you read chapter 24, would you like to volunteer for Ezekiel's mission? Keep in mind, he was a real person with real emotions.

Watching his wife die, then being forced to carry on as though nothing has happened, is the price of being God's spokesman. Sometimes we think obedience to God leads to a path of blessings and happiness. Nothing could be further from the truth. Following God's plan for our lives brings rewards, but it also comes with a price.

When Ezekiel addresses the nations around Israel and Judah, he devotes the most space to the Phoenician city of Tyre. The city, on the coast of modern Lebanon, was a prosperous trading center throughout the ancient world. Its ships established trade and colonies in Spain and North Africa and sailed throughout the Red Sea, Indian Ocean, and as far as Britain. The ancient city of Carthage was a Phoenician colony that challenged Rome for supremacy just before the time of Christ. Carthage nearly defeated Rome through the cunning of its greatest general, Hannibal. Chapter 28, which addresses the king of Tyre, is thought by many to describe the rise and fall of Satan himself.

Ezekiel 29–32

Why do the prophets have so much to say to Egypt? Egypt and Israel are natural allies. We see this even today. Egypt was the first Arab nation to make, and keep, peace with modern Israel. Solomon married Pharaoh's daughter and secured his horses from Egypt's stables. The Jews turned to Egypt for help when threatened by Assyria and Babylon. In Jeremiah we read that many of the people left behind by Nebuchadnezzar fled to Egypt instead of staying in the land and suffering under God's judgment. Several centuries after Jeremiah, a large Jewish population lived in the Egyptian city of Alexandria and even built a replica of the temple there. Even after the coming of

Christ, Egypt played a key role in God's work. The church in Alexandria was one of the strongest in the early centuries.

Ezekiel 33–37

Before you read chapter 33, read Matthew 28:19-20 and Acts 1:8. How does our calling to be witnesses for Christ relate to Ezekiel's call to be a watchman for Israel? Also, compare chapter 34 to John 10. The good shepherd God promises through Ezekiel will ultimately be filled by Jesus. Ezekiel 36:26-27 also finds its fulfillment in the New Testament. Compare it to 2 Corinthians 5:17. Notice also how chapter 37 points toward Christ.

Ezekiel 38–48

Some commentators try to equate Gog with Russia, but nothing in the Bible leads to that conclusion. The two names, Gog and Magog, are symbolic, representing the forces of evil and Satan. These chapters reassure us that no matter how fierce the Enemy's attack, God will always prevail. His victory will be both overwhelming and complete. We therefore have nothing to fear, for if God is for us, who can be against us?

Beginning with chapter 40, Ezekiel describes the centerpiece of a restored Israel: the new temple. Yet this temple will never actually be built. Since Christ will end the need for sacrifices, it is probably best to understand chapters 40–48 as symbolic language. Ezekiel describes the time when Israel will be restored, and what is the single most important part of that restoration? Worship and the people's relationship with the Lord. Ezekiel doesn't describe rebuilt walls of Jerusalem, which people in that day would think of as a priority. Instead, he describes the rebuilt walls around the Lord's sanctuary. The place will be holy with a river of healing flowing out of it (47:1-12). Compare this to the promise of Revelation 22. Most important of all, the Lord's glory returns. He reclaims his people as his own, and he will dwell in their presence forever and ever. The vision of the new temple gives the exiles the promises we take for granted when we think of Christ's return, yet Ezekiel describes it with words and images they can understand. The ultimate fulfillment of these chapters awaits the day the sky splits and Jesus returns.

The Minor Prophets

The central question of the Bible, the central question of all of human history, is simply: Who is God? The question, which sounds irrelevant to postmodern ears, is the single most important issue with which any of us will wrestle. Human beings were made to know and serve God. Everything else we do on this earth passes away and is soon forgotten. Yet the way we serve God lasts forever. If we were made to know and serve God, the question we must then ask ourselves is: Who is he?

Once we come to Christ, we might think we have this puzzle solved. However, even though we might know which God is real, do we really know the God who is real? We might be able to pick him out of a lineup, but do we know his heart, his passion, and his character? Do we understand how he thinks and how he works? These are the questions the twelve Minor Prophets answer. They bring us face-to-face with the character of God. They do more than pronounce judgment on sinful people. They put God on display in a way we've never seen before. This truth hits us from the beginning of the very first book.

Hosea

Jesus told parables. Hosea lives his. God tells the prophet to marry a prostitute and to have children with her that may or may not be his. In this way Hosea lives out the drama of God's relationship with his people. Hosea plays the part of God, and Gomer, his wife, plays the part of Israel. Just as Gomer runs after other lovers, Israel has prostituted itself to other gods. The idea of idolatry as prostitution isn't completely a spiritual or symbolic concept. Part of the worship of Baal and Asherah involves having sex with temple prostitutes. This act of "worship" is supposed to induce the fertility gods to send rain so the crops would grow. By living out this parable, Hosea reveals God as the scorned lover who still loves the bride who left him for other men. His love is so great that he will one day take her back and restore her as his bride.

Hosea was a prophet to the northern kingdom, which was known as Israel, Samaria, or Ephraim. These ten tribes rejected Solomon's son, Rehoboam, to form the northern kingdom. Never in their history did they serve the Lord alone. They fell into idol worship from the moment their first king, Jeroboam, built two golden calves and placed them in the cities of Bethel and Dan. The Jeroboam mentioned in Hosea 1:1 is the second king by this name. Hosea prophesied from around 743 BC to shortly before the fall of the north in 721 BC. He lived and spoke around the same time as Isaiah, Amos, and Micah.

One of the key verses in the book is 6:6. It echoes Micah 6:8. Hosea writes, "I want you to be merciful; I don't want your sacrifices. I want you to know God; that's more important than burnt offerings." These words reveal God's heart and show all he is looking for in his bride. Sadly, Israel never wants to know God and couldn't care less about mercy. This is really the theme of the book. God loves, but the object of his love is completely indifferent to him.

Joel

Joel, unlike the other prophets, doesn't give us any details as to where or when he lived. Most of the prophets begin by listing the kings who reigned during their ministry. Joel does not. Some commentators believe his lack of reference to a king means he preached after the Jews came back from their exile in Babylon. Others place the date of his book around 837 BC, when the boy Joash reigned as king. Either way, his message still focuses on the power and sovereignty of God, who will judge his people. Interwoven is the hope for future restoration that goes beyond rebuilt walls. In Joel we hear the promise that someday God himself will dwell in all his children through his Spirit. We take this promise for granted, because the Holy Spirit now lives within all believers and makes us God's temples (1 Corinthians 6:19). Peter quotes Joel on the day of Pentecost, when the Holy Spirit comes upon every believer for the very first time.

Amos 1–5

Amos is the least likely prophet. He was a fig farmer and a shepherd, not a trained, professional prophet. Although he preached in the northern kingdom, he was from the south. He lived around the same time as Isaiah. In Amos we discover God's love for justice and his concern for the oppressed. The people of Israel not only worship false gods, but their judges make decisions based on bribes, the poor are denied justice, and the rich keep getting richer at their expense. Chapter 4 describes the incremental judgment God will send to get the people's attention. Because they won't listen, Amos tells them, "Prepare to meet your God" (4:12). Chilling words.

The key passage is 5:21-24, which says, "I hate all your show and pretense—the hypocrisy of your religious festivals and solemn assemblies. I will not accept your burnt offerings and grain offerings. I won't even notice all your choice peace offerings. Away with your hymns of praise! They are only noise to my ears. I will not listen to your music, no matter how lovely it is. Instead, I want to see a mighty flood of justice, a river of righteous living that will never run dry." These verses remind us of the connection between worship and righteous living. Religious talk doesn't mean anything if it isn't translated into obeying God and sharing his passion.

Amos 6–9

Amos 6 describes the luxury of the people of Samaria. They are rich and powerful, yet a day is coming when God will hold them accountable for all they have done. Chapter 7 presents a powerful picture of God standing with a plumb line with which he will measure his people. The image sounds much like the New Testament's description of the Final Judgment, when every mouth will be silenced. No one will be able to complain that God isn't fair because the plumb line of his requirements will be plain for all to see. Amos ends with promises of restoration. Although God will punish his people, his love for them never ends.

Obadiah

Obadiah is one of the shortest books in the Bible. He wrote these words shortly after Jerusalem fell in 586 BC, which makes him a contemporary of Jeremiah. He directs the twenty-one verses of his prophecy at the nation of Edom. As you may remember, Edom descended from Jacob's brother, Esau. Yet instead of helping Jacob's descendants when they needed it the most, Edom stood by and watched Israel and Judah be destroyed. They then swept in to plunder what was left behind. Because of this, they too will stand before God and be judged. The book shows us how we must show mercy to those who suffer, even when their suffering is justified. We can't kick people when they're down, nor should we rejoice at our enemies' downfall. Compare this idea to Galatians 6:1-2.

Jonah

Thanks to *VeggieTales*, we know about the reluctant prophet who is swallowed by a whale. He runs away from God when the Lord tells him to go and preach to Israel's enemy (and ultimate conqueror) Assyria. The events of the book take place between forty and sixty years before the fall of the northern kingdom, or around 785–760 BC.

Yet this story is about more than a reluctant prophet. As you read, note the contrast between Jonah's and God's heart. The Lord longs to have people turn to him, even the vile and wicked people who live in Nineveh. In this book we see God as compassionate and eager to forgive. We also see ourselves in Jonah. We aren't so eager for God to forgive people who have hurt us. God loves people far more than we ever will, and far more than we give him credit for. Jonah dispels the myth that God is distant and hard to please. God has his arms open wide, begging people to come to him and find forgiveness and life. This is a book about God's grace and the compulsion many of us believers feel to hoard that grace for ourselves rather than share it with others.

Micah

Micah lived and preached around the same time as Isaiah. Reading the two, you will find some parallel thoughts. Micah lays the blame for the nation's demise on its leaders. The prophets will say anything if someone pays them enough beer, and the political leaders use their position to fleece the people. As 3:11 puts it,

> You rulers govern for the bribes you can get; you priests teach God's laws only for a price; you prophets won't prophesy unless you are paid. Yet all of you claim you are

depending on the LORD. "No harm can come to us," you say, "for the LORD is here among us."

Micah is about as subtle as a sledgehammer. He too echoes God's concern for the poor and oppressed. Micah also focuses on the future. He points toward the coming of the Messiah and his eternal reign. In that time, the Lord's temple will become the most important place on earth (4:1). Micah shows that Israel's future restoration is about far more than that nation. Someday God will cause the promises he made to Abraham to come true, and all the nations of the earth will be blessed by his descendants. Micah lets us know there is more to the story of God than we've read so far, leaving us ready and eager for the New Testament.

Nahum

The book of Nahum is the follow-up to Jonah. The spiritual awakening Jonah's preaching spawned eventually died out. Assyria returned to its bloodthirsty ways. Wealthy and powerful, for a time the Assyrians were the most envied nation in the ancient Near East—and the most hated. Assyria set a standard for cruelty few have equaled since. And God held them accountable for it.

Nahum, like Jonah, speaks to the capital city of Nineveh. Prophesying around 660 to 650 BC, he tells the Assyrians destruction is coming. The city of lies and murder will soon be plundered, all her wealth carried off. And no one will shed a tear. The news of her downfall will cause the rest of the world to applaud with joy. Those who never showed mercy will find none when their time comes.

Nahum shows how God actively participates in history. The Lord watches not only the actions of individuals, but also nations, and he holds us accountable for what we do. A day is coming when he will set things right and dispense justice. This knowledge gives us hope as we suffer for Christ. Someday all the wrongdoers will have to answer to God. But it should also be a word of warning as we look at the world around us. God judges nations for their actions, and that judgment doesn't wait for the end of time. What does he see when he looks at our nation?

Habakkuk

If God is in control, why do the wicked prosper while the righteous suffer? And when suffering comes on the Lord's people at the hands of people who scoff at the very idea of God, how are we supposed to respond? These questions run through the short book of Habakkuk. They don't just trouble the prophet who preached around 600 BC, they still plague us today. Why do the wicked prosper? Why doesn't God do something? Is he even listening when we scream for help?

Habakkuk preached around the same time as Jeremiah, but the similarities don't stop there. Both books overflow with passion and pain. You can hear the agony in Habakkuk's voice as he cries out to God. And Habakkuk, like Jeremiah, complains to God about all he sees unfolding around him. "Is your plan in all of this to wipe us out?" he shouts (1:12). He doesn't have to wait long for an answer. The book is a conversation between Habakkuk and God as the Babylonians are invading Judah.

Habakkuk 2:4 could be called the theme verse of the New Testament. It describes how we can live a life that pleases God. Romans 1:17, Galatians 3:11, and Hebrews 10:38 all quote it. The verse is even stronger when you see it in the context of Habakkuk's life. His world is falling apart. The Babylonian army is attacking. All around him are death and destruction and confusion. He wonders where God is and why he doesn't do something.

And this is God's reply: "Trust me. Live by faith." Even when the evidence around us screams that God has turned his back on us, trust him. That's what it means to live by faith. The third chapter expands this idea even more, especially verses 17-19.

Zephaniah

Few of us tremble at the thought of the horrors of prison life. Except for the rare occasion when we watch a prison movie, a wave of fear doesn't sweep over us at the prospect of being locked up. When we obey the law, we don't worry about punishment. But when we don't, we do. Perhaps we see a highway patrol car and look down to find our speedometer reading eighty miles per hour. Then we worry. A cold sweat runs down the back of our neck. The feeling may still come when we're going sixty-five, but it doesn't last. We know we have nothing to fear when we keep the speed limit.

In essence, that's what Zephaniah says. He prophesied during the reign of King Josiah, around 640 BC. Josiah was a good king, but his father, Manasseh, was the worst of the worst. That simply made him fit in with the people of Judah. By this point of reading the Prophets, you are familiar with the nation's sins.

Zephaniah calls the nation back to God. He tells those who fear the Lord to humble themselves before God and pray. Perhaps then they will be spared. But he knows they won't, because so many people "sit contented in their sins, indifferent to the LORD, thinking he will do nothing at all to them" (1:12). These are the ones God will search out with a lantern. He has had enough. Zephaniah makes it clear this isn't what God wants to do. "I have wiped out many nations. . . . Surely they will have reverence for me now! Surely they will listen to my warnings, so I won't need to strike again" (3:6-7). But the people won't. Since they won't let go of their idols, God will now pry those idols out of their hands.

Haggai

Haggai never talks about getting rid of idols, nor does he make lengthy predictions of coming judgment. His message is different because this is a different time. God's judgment swept across the land, and the people were exiled to Babylon for seventy years. Then the Babylonian Empire fell to the Persians, and the Persian King Cyrus issued a proclamation allowing the captives to go home. Most stayed put in Babylon, but a handful went back to the Promised Land and started over. These are the people to whom God sends Haggai to prophesy, eighteen years after the first wave of refugees returned.

The return to the Promised Land is very different from the first time the Jews took possession of it. They haven't returned as conquerors. Instead, they are trickling in as refugees. Ten of the tribes have disappeared after being absorbed by Assyria two hundred years earlier. By the time of Haggai's prophecy, the Jews have reestablished a government and civil order but remain a weak vassal state under Persia. The people are beaten down, afraid, defeated.

God sends his prophet with a simple message: "I am with you, says the LORD!" (1:13). He hasn't forgotten his promises, and he can never forget his people. But he also has a command: Rebuild the temple. The Babylonian army tore the temple apart and carried off the sacred objects. That doesn't matter to God. Now is the time for the people to rebuild the temple and get on with the business of worshiping him. That's why he called them to himself. What are they waiting for?

Zechariah 1–7

Zechariah is a contemporary of Haggai. The first half of his book reassures the Jews that God hasn't forgotten them. In fact, his love for them is stronger than ever. He plans to bless Jerusalem and fill it with his presence. Then the entire world will see God's love and passion for his people.

But the people also have a responsibility. Zechariah echoes Haggai's call to rebuild the temple. He also urges the people to turn away from sin. Learn the lessons from the past, he urges. Don't repeat the mistakes of your forefathers, he cries. Idolatry isn't the issue. Justice and mercy are. Verses 7:8-9 sound a lot like the book of James, which says, "Pure and lasting religion in the sight of God our Father means that we must care for orphans and widows in their troubles, and refuse to let the world corrupt us" (1:27).

Pay particular attention to chapter 7. Apparently the Jews commemorate the day the temple was destroyed by making the anniversary an annual day of mourning and fasting. Yet notice God's reaction to this. He points out that they are mourning for the wrong person. They look at this tragic event as a blow against their nation, as though *they* were the injured party. God tells them to think again. Instead of thinking about themselves, they should think about him. The temple was destroyed for the same reason the nation was judged, because the people had turned their backs on God. The real tragedy wasn't the Babylonians burning down the temple Solomon built, but God's people acting as though he was irrelevant. Zechariah reminds us that this life is not about us, but God.

Zechariah 8–14

The second half of Zechariah looks beyond the year 480 BC into the future. These chapters describe both the first and second comings of Jesus. You will see several prophecies directly related to Christ. Chapter 9 describes the day Jesus rode into Jerusalem in triumph, less than a week before his crucifixion. Verse 12:10 also refers to Christ's death. Intermixed through the rest of these chapters are promises that lie in the future. Many have yet to be fulfilled.

In some ways these chapters are like the book of Revelation. The four horses referred to throughout the book are also found in Revelation 6. The last couple of chapters of Zechariah sound like the last few chapters of Revelation. Both point to a time when Christ will return and establish his throne on the earth. Keep this in mind as you read Zechariah 8–14. It will help these last chapters make sense.

Malachi

One of the more troubling passages in the Bible is Malachi 1:2-3. The NIV renders it, "Yet I have loved Jacob, but Esau I have hated." If God loves the entire world, how can he hate Esau? The NLT uses the word "rejected" instead of hated, which makes the meaning of the Hebrew word clearer. However, the bottom line is this: Before either Jacob or Esau was born, God chose Jacob as the vessel through whom he would build his nation through which the entire world would be blessed. Esau, on the other hand, God rejected. If that doesn't sound fair, it is because it isn't, but not for the reason you might think. When you think back on their lives, neither Jacob nor Esau did anything to commend himself to God. God wasn't fair to Jacob. He gave him mercy. Esau, on the other hand, received justice. But shouldn't God give each one an equal opportunity to find forgiveness and grace? Read Romans 9 for the answer. As you do, keep this in mind: Because God is God, he can do whatever he wants, and he never has to explain himself to anyone. That's part of what makes him God, not us.

Malachi ends with a promise, the last promise made in the Old Testament. Not surprisingly, the last promise made in the Old Testament is the first fulfilled in the New. It is the promise to send "Elijah" to prepare the way for the Lord. John the Baptist came because of this promise. His message from God sounds like Malachi's: "I am the LORD, and I do not change. . . . Return to me, and I will return to you" (3:6-7). Twenty-four hundred years later, the need for this message is as great as ever.

The Writings

Psalms, Job, Proverbs,
Ruth, Song of Solomon,
Ecclesiastes, Lamentations,
Esther, Daniel, Ezra, Nehemiah,
First and Second Chronicles

AUTHORS

The Writings were penned by a variety of people over a period of several hundred years. Some books had a single author, while Psalms and Proverbs were collections of many people's writings. David wrote most of the psalms. Solomon penned most of Proverbs, along with Song of Solomon and Ecclesiastes. The prophet Jeremiah probably wrote Lamentations, and Daniel wrote the book that bears his name. Nehemiah is written in the first person, which implies he penned the book that bears his name. Jewish tradition says Ezra wrote Ezra and Chronicles, although the books don't mention their writer by name. In the same way, Job, Ruth, and Esther are silent as to who their authors were.

WHEN WERE THESE BOOKS WRITTEN?

Parts of these books were written throughout Israel's history. Job is probably the oldest book, perhaps dating from the time of Abraham (1600–2000 BC), while Ezra, Nehemiah, and 1 and 2 Chronicles were written a little more than four hundred years before the birth of Jesus.

WHAT ARE THEY ABOUT?

After reading the Law and the Prophets, you now know Israel's story. You know how God made this nation, what happened to them, and why it happened. The Writings complete this picture by giving us the human element. They take us inside the lives of those who lived through these experiences and show us how to live for the Lord in a fallen world. They guide us through a broad range of emotions and circumstances and thoughts we will experience as we live by faith.

The books of the Writings are very different from one another. Psalms is a collection of songs. Proverbs is a series of wise sayings passed down from Solomon and others. The Song of Solomon is a series of love songs celebrating romance while never mentioning God. Some of the books read like books of history. One, Daniel, also contains some of the most vivid apocalyptic prophecies this side of Revelation. No book matches the raw emotion of Job as he wrestles with questions that go to the heart of trusting God. The Writings also include the book that speaks to postmodern culture as if it had been written last week: Ecclesiastes. The books' order may seem random. It isn't. As you read, you will see how the books go together.

Psalms

Plot: How to worship. The Psalms are a collection of songs and prayers for worship both as individuals and as a group. They include songs of praise, laments (cries of distress and mourning), wisdom psalms that teach, royal psalms from the king, and songs of thanksgiving. The different types of psalms are scattered throughout the book. The psalms were meant to be sung, although the original music has not been passed down to us.

Key characters: The characters in this book are the writers. David wrote more psalms than anyone else. Other writers include Asaph, the man King David put in charge of the temple musicians; the sons of Korah, who were a group of temple singers; Moses; and Solomon. Many of the psalms name no writer.

Job

Plot: Why do you serve God? The question drives this story of a righteous and godly man who loses everything he owns and everything precious to him in one day. The book builds on the question of why we love God. It dares to ask: Does God have to bless us to keep our affection? Most of the book is a conversation between Job and three men who come to comfort him. The book ends with God speaking directly to Job. From beginning to end, the book defies all formulas about faith and God.

Key characters: God, Satan, Job, Eliphaz, Bildad, Zophar, Elihu

Turning point in the story: Job 28

Proverbs

Plot: How to live wisely in a fallen world. Proverbs is a collection of proverbs, or wise sayings. It touches on everything from how to know the Lord, to how to impart wisdom to our children, to how to avoid foolish mistakes.

Key characters: The writer, Solomon. Chapter 30 was written by Agur, son of Jakeh, and 31 was written by Lemuel, the king of Massa. If those names sound unfamiliar to you, you are in good company. The rest of the Bible says very little about them.

Ruth

Plot: The story of Ruth, a woman from the country of Moab, who marries a man from the tribe of Judah. The book tells of her unselfish love for her mother-in-law after Ruth's husband died and how God takes care of both of them. It then develops into a love story between Ruth and Boaz. Ruth was King David's great-grandmother, even though she was a Moabite.

Key characters: Ruth, Naomi, Boaz

Turning point in the story: Ruth 3

Song of Solomon

Plot: How to love. The Song of Solomon is a series of love songs that celebrate romance. Some are graphic, although their graphic nature is sometimes lost on modern audiences. Some images that seemed sexy three thousand years ago (like comparing a woman's neck to a tower) don't work today, while others are timeless.

Key characters: Solomon, his bride

Ecclesiastes

Plot: What is the point of life?
Key character: The author, King Solomon
Turning point in the story: Ecclesiastes 12:13-14

Lamentations

Plot: A series of songs mourning the fall of Jerusalem
Key characters: God, those suffering under his judgment
Turning point in the story: Lamentations 3:19-24

Esther

Plot: The story takes place during the rule of the Persian Empire. Some Jews have returned from exile to the Promised Land, but many thousands remain in the regions where the Babylonians sent them. This story tells of a Jewish woman, Esther, who becomes the queen of Persia while keeping her ethnicity a secret. A plot arises that threatens to wipe out all the Jews. Esther risks her life to save her people. Even today, the Jewish people continue to celebrate the events of this book in their Feast of Purim.
Key characters: Esther, Mordecai, Haman, King Xerxes
Turning point in the story: Esther 6

Daniel

Plot: The book combines the story of Daniel, a young man carried off with the first group of exiles to Babylon, with his apocalyptic prophecies. The first half of the book is primarily Daniel's story, along with that of his friends Shadrach, Meshach, and Abednego. The second half is mostly prophecies. The tone and style of Daniel's prophecies are very different from those in the other prophetic books. Chapters 7–12 are most like the book of Revelation.

Key characters: Daniel, Shadrach, Meshach, Abednego, Nebuchadnezzar

Turning point in the story: Daniel 1:8

Ezra–Nehemiah

Plot: Although they are two books in our Bible, the two are one in the Hebrew Bible. Together they take us back to the Promised Land with the exiles who returned there. Ezra tells how the temple was rebuilt and the people turned to the Lord. Nehemiah records the rebuilding of Jerusalem's walls and the removal of the people's shame as a defeated nation.

Key characters: Ezra, Nehemiah

Turning point in the story: Nehemiah 2

First and Second Chronicles

Plot: Together the books retell Israel's story, beginning with Adam. Most of 1 Chronicles reads like a family tree. However, for the Jews after the exile, this list is important. It allows them to see God's faithfulness. The family tree also shows the nation's unity and its role in history. The story picks up in earnest with David and continues on through Cyrus's decree that the Jews could go back home after seventy years in exile. Unlike 1 and 2 Kings, the chronicler basically ignores the northern kingdom.

Key characters: David, Solomon, Hezekiah, Josiah

Turning point in the story: 2 Chronicles 10

Psalms

The book of Psalms could be called the songbook of ancient Israel. Yet that would be like calling the *Mona Lisa* a painting or the Beatles a band from Liverpool. While technically correct, it hardly begins to tell the story. The psalms were meant to be sung as Israel gathered together to worship the Lord at the temple. But the book of Psalms is more than a hymnal. The songs and prayers express the heights and depths of a living relationship with the Sovereign Lord of the universe. Building on the foundation of the Law, the psalms show obedience is more than simply keeping a set of rules found in the Law. Instead, it overflows with passion for the one true God.

Since Moses wrote at least one of them, the psalms date back as far as 1400 BC. One or two could have been written after the Exile. Most were written during the time of David. The book of Psalms is divided into five books. Book One consists of Psalms 1–41; Two is 42–72; Three 73–89; Four 90–106; and Psalms 107–150 make up Book Five. David wrote many of the psalms. Thirty-seven of the forty-one psalms in Book One are attributed to him. Eighteen of the thirty-one in Book Two list David as the author, one lists Solomon, and the rest are anonymous. Only one psalm is attributed to David in Book Three, two in Book Four, and fifteen in Book Five.

Psalms 1–7

The psalms are Hebrew poetry. Rather than using rhymes to tie lines together, Hebrew poetry repeats thoughts. You can see this in the second psalm:

> Why do the nations conspire
> and the peoples plot in vain?

The kings of the earth take their stand
and the rulers gather together
against the Lord
and against his Anointed One.
"Let us break their chains," they say,
"and throw off their fetters." (Psalm 2:1-3, NIV)

This repetition of thought forms the rhythm of the psalms. At times the psalmist will repeat one line over and over as a refrain or song chorus. All of these songs were meant to be sung.

Psalm 2 also shows how worried God is about the twists and turns of politics on earth. This psalm is a welcome reminder of how God is in control, regardless of what happens in the capitals of the world.

Psalms 8–13

These psalms emphasize God's majesty and power. He sits on his throne in heaven, but nothing on earth escapes his notice. When bad things happen, don't worry. The Lord is in his holy temple. He still rules from heaven (11:4). We need these reassurances because he sometimes seems so far away. In life, it sometimes feels as though God is hiding when we need him the most (10:1). But he isn't far away. He sees the violence done to the helpless, and he hears the groans of the poor. He will rise up to rescue us because his promises never fail (12:5). Until he does, he calls us to trust him and rejoice in his unfailing love (13:5).

Psalms 14–18

The brief titles on many of the psalms usually say nothing more than, "A Psalm of David." A few mention the tune of the song or the instruments to be played. But once in a while the title tells us when and why David wrote the song. Psalm 18 does this. David wrote these words on the day the Lord rescued him from Saul and his other enemies. The entire psalm can also be found in 2 Samuel 22.

Psalms 19–22

After you read Psalm 22, turn to the story of the cross in Matthew 27. As Jesus hangs dying for you and me, he cries out to his Father, "My God, my God, why have you forsaken me?" (verse 46). In his moment of anguish and grief, Jesus quotes Psalm 22. The words of David ring in his ears. Yet, as you read the psalm, you see the same process in reverse. The psalm sounds as though David is standing at the foot of the cross watching his future Savior die. This is an example of a prophetic psalm that was fulfilled in Christ.

Psalms 23–27

You may be able to quote Psalm 23 without reading it again. If so, slow down. Read the psalm in a Bible version that isn't as familiar. Try to listen to the words as though you are hearing them for the very first time. This psalm is more than a comforting poem to pull out in times of crisis. David expresses his total dependence on the Lord. Listen to his words. You will hear him describe the essence of what it means to walk with the Lord by faith.

Psalms 28–32

Psalm 32 takes us through the painful process of confessing our sin to God and experiencing his cleansing. First John 1:9 promises God will forgive our sins when we confess. Psalm 32 shows this means more than admitting the obvious to God and saying, "I did it, you caught me." Confession that leads to forgiveness and a restored relationship with God comes from a heart broken over what we have done. We aren't just sorry we've been caught. Instead, we are crushed because we've harmed God and treated his name with contempt. Anything less may be an admittance of guilt, but it doesn't demonstrate the changed heart that wants nothing more to do with sin.

Psalms 33–37
David wrote Psalm 34 at one of the lowest points of his life. Yet he starts by singing, "I will praise the LORD at all times. I will constantly speak his praises." How can he talk about praising God when he has to pretend to be insane to save his life? He's been driven out of Israel by Saul. This former hero is now an outlaw. Things are so bad, he runs off to Israel's mortal enemy, the Philistines, because he knows this is the one place King Saul won't follow him. Yet David has made his name by killing Philistines in times of war. That's why he has to pretend to be insane. He is alone. Rejected. Despised. No place to turn. And yet he writes, "I will praise the LORD at all times. . . ." Amazing.

Psalms 38–41
These four psalms all expose David's deep emotions as he cries out to God. Each psalm is personal. They depart from the false formula that says God always blesses the righteous. We find David struggling, wondering where God is and why he doesn't act. Yet, in spite of his circumstances, he continues to cling to the Lord by faith. He knows no matter what happens, God will not forget his children. Verse 40:17 expresses this confidence with simple eloquence: "As for me, I am poor and needy, but

the Lord is thinking about me right now. You are my helper and savior. Do not delay, O my God."

Psalms 42–46
Book Two opens with Psalms 42–43, which are one psalm in the original text. The first eight psalms of this section were written by the "sons of Korah." These were Levites who were the temple gatekeepers (1 Chronicles 9:19). Their names are also included among the musicians David appointed to lead the nation in worship when it gathered together (1 Chronicles 6:31-37). Asaph, the author of several psalms, was also one of the temple musicians.

Psalms 47–51
Psalm 51 is David's response to God after the prophet Nathan confronted him after his sin with Bathsheba. The full story can be found in 2 Samuel 11–12. At least a year passed from the moment David looked down from his rooftop to see Bathsheba taking a bath until the Lord sent Nathan to David. This psalm gives us a few insights into what that year was like for David. His joy had disappeared while his acts haunted him. David knew the Law and he knew God. While outwardly he could act like everything was fine, inside his soul, a battle raged. David's confession consists of more than words. Notice how forgiveness and worship and evangelism go together. As David experiences God's salvation, he sings his praises and tells others of the greatness of God.

Psalms 52–57
David wrote four of these six psalms while Saul was trying to hunt him down and kill him. Try to put yourself in his place as

you read his prayers. He knows God has anointed him as the next king. But the current king, his father-in-law, wants him dead. David can't hide in Israel because people's devotion to the throne caused many to betray him. Where can he turn? Think about the turmoil he must feel. If God is for him, why is the whole world against him?

Psalms 58–62

Psalm 60 comes on the heels of a great victory, but it doesn't sound like it. David speaks of the weakness of the army and describes their defenses as broken. He cries out for God to come and rescue him. What does this say about David and his view of his military victories? And what does it say about David's dependence upon God?

Psalms 63–68

Blaise Pascal said every human being has a God-shaped hole within his or her soul. All of us were created to know and worship God, and we will never be satisfied until we do. Psalm 63 describes this hole in the life of a believer. David wrote this psalm in the desert of Judah, a region that receives fewer than ten inches of rain per year. He compares his physical thirst for water to his far more intense longing for God. This is the mark of one who truly loves God. This powerful psalm challenges all of us to a deeper devotion to the Lord.

Psalms 69–72

The last psalm of Book Two ends with these words: "This ends the prayers of David son of Jesse." Yet they come as the last verse of a psalm attributed to Solomon. How do these two go together? It may be that Psalm 72 was written by David for Solomon as he took his father's throne. The transfer of power took place while David was still alive, which insured that David's choice became king. He had many sons by several different wives. More than one of them thought he should be the next king. David ended the arguing by handpicking Solomon and crowning him before he died. This psalm may be David's blessing for his son.

Psalms 73–77

Psalm 73 describes one of the most difficult tests of faith we will face. Asaph looked around one day and noticed the easy life of people who couldn't care less about God. Most of us hope the wicked will always be miserable, but that isn't the case. As Asaph pointed out, these proud people who thumbed their noses at God were wealthy and didn't have a trouble in the world. The longer he watched, the more a question rattled around in his head: "Was it for nothing that I have kept my heart pure and kept myself from doing wrong?" Simply put, he is asking if this life of faith is worth it.

Psalm 73 is the answer. This psalm is the perfect remedy for the envy we often feel for those who have it all. It moves our focus beyond the few short years we live on this earth. When we see life from God's perspective, we discover the trouble is worth it. The psalm also shows how we must deal with the bitterness toward God that our envy of others can cause. In the end, when we allow God to move our eyes from this world to the world to come, we too will tell everyone the wonderful things God does for us.

Psalms 78–80

How do you teach the truths of God to people who can't read or don't have access to books? This problem confronted the leaders of ancient Israel. The book, as we think of it today, did not exist. The Scriptures were written on scrolls, which were usually made of animal skin. Needless to say, they were expensive to produce and not very portable. Therefore, the average Israelite living in Kadesh-Barnea couldn't pull the Bible off his bookshelf and read it. Yet Israel's survival as a people depended on their living by the Word of God. How then could they learn the Word when they didn't have access to books?

Psalm 78 tells how. Asaph puts the story of Israel to music and teaches it to the people as a song. The more they sing the song, the more these truths of God sink into the people's souls. This is far more than a song of worship. Like many of the psalms by Asaph, it was designed to teach the people about the Lord in order that they might live for him.

Psalms 81–85

The Lord's dwelling place found in Psalm 84:1 doesn't refer to heaven. Remember, the sons of Korah were the gatekeepers at the temple. The Lord's dwelling place in ancient Israel was the temple. The psalm doesn't speak of a desire to go to heaven but of the longing to enter into the Lord's presence and worship him here on earth. Verse 10 is therefore more than a romantic notion. The writer is a gatekeeper in the house of his God. He's devoted his life to serving the Lord. Instead of looking around at the life he could have had, he focuses on the wonder of being allowed to spend every day in God's presence. He concludes, "A single day in your courts is better than a thousand anywhere else!" This was more than a line in a song. It was his life.

Psalms 86–89

Psalms 86–87 both express a truth the Jews never fully grasped. All the nations of the world are part of God's plan.

We take this for granted today. After all, the average church is almost entirely made up of people who were not born Jews. The thought that God's plan of salvation might not extend to us seems ridiculous. Yet the Jews never quite grasped this mystery. We find allusions to the promise in God's covenant with Abraham and in the writings of the prophets, but the idea never became mainstream Jewish thought. Psalms 86–87 foretell what finally became reality when Peter went to Cornelius's house and shared with him the good news of Jesus (Acts 10–11).

Psalms 90–94

Book Four is unusual in that all but three of its psalms are anonymous. Moses is listed as the author of the first, and David wrote two others. The rest could have been written by anyone. The fact that so many of the psalms name no human author reminds us that the power of Scripture lies not in the human authors, but in the God who inspired their writing. Perhaps the reason so few names appear in Book Four lies in its focus. The psalms in this section focus on worship. They sing the praises of our God and call us to join in the song. Even if we knew who wrote each one, we would forget the moment we allowed these songs to carry us into God's presence.

Psalms 95–102

These psalms teach us how to worship. Together they emphasize the Lord's power as the one true God. They also speak of his glory and honor and majesty. The mountains melt away from his presence while the heavens sing his praises. "Come let us sing to the Lord," the psalms exhort us again and again. Some call us to sing a new song to the Lord for the wonderful things he has done. Worship is never static, nor do God's miracles all lie in the past. We need to continually sing his praises and remember everything he does today. As God does something new, the songs must become new. The point is clear: Worship is to be a lifestyle for those who walk by faith. Songs of praise and thanksgiving should continually flow from our mouths.

Psalms 103–106

Psalm 103:13-14 says, "The LORD is like a father to his children, tender and compassionate to those who fear him. For he understands how weak we are; he knows we are only dust." When the Bible talks about God as our Father, this is the image it draws upon. Tender, compassionate, understanding, he is the perfect father.

Psalm 104 draws a different image of God. The psalm looks at creation in light of its Creator. In this psalm we see all of nature working exactly the way God designed it in his wisdom. How different this view is from one that imagines the world as the end result of a series of random events.

Psalms 107–110

David wrote Psalm 110, but he wasn't talking about himself in it. These verses tell us about the Messiah. Jesus used Psalm 110 to confound the Pharisees. In this psalm David calls the coming Messiah "Lord." Jesus asked the Pharisees how the Messiah could be a son of David if David called him Lord. The question might puzzle you as much as it did the Pharisees, but the answer lies in Jesus himself. He came as a descendant of David, but he was greater than David. And the ancient king recognized this when he penned Psalm 110.

Psalms 111–118

When Jesus came, his people rejected him. God sent his Son to the Jews as their Messiah, but they crucified him instead. The apostles explained why this was a necessary part of God's plan by quoting Psalm 118:22-23:

> The stone rejected by the builders
> has now become the cornerstone.
> This is the LORD's doing,
> and it is marvelous to see.

Their use of the psalm shows more than the prophetic nature of some of the psalms. It also demonstrates how Jesus' followers interpreted the events taking place around them through the filter of the Bible. Simply put, they thought biblically. They possessed a biblical worldview.

Psalm 119

Psalm 119 is the longest chapter in the Bible, 176 verses. This psalm was written as an acrostic poem, where each line of all twenty-two paragraphs begins with a different letter of the Hebrew alphabet. Verses 1-8 all begin with aleph (a), verses 9-16 begin with beth (b), and so on through the 176 verses. What sets the psalm apart is its focus. The song celebrates the Word of God. It shows both the power of the Word and the attitude every believer should have toward it. In effect, Psalm 119 answers the question: Why should I devote large blocks of my time to studying God's Word?

Psalms 120–134

These fifteen short psalms are songs of ascent. Pilgrims going to Jerusalem for the Passover, Feast of Weeks, or Day of

Atonement sang these songs as they traveled. All are anonymous, and at least one was probably written after the Exile. The songs celebrate God's power and love and call worshipers to trust in him with all their hearts.

Psalms 135–136

These two psalms celebrate all God did for his people in the past. Notice the refrain of Psalm 136, "His faithful love endures forever." The Hebrew term translated "faithful love" is the word *chesed*. The word carries the idea of mercy and undeserved kindness. It is one of the most important words in the Hebrew Bible, for it describes the love, grace, and mercy God pours out on his children. Psalm 136 reminds us God's *chesed* lasts forever and ever. Paul builds on this idea as he writes, "And I am convinced that nothing can ever separate us from his love" (Romans 8:38).

Psalms 137–143

Psalm 137 was written much later than most of the other psalms. The unknown writer penned it either while still in exile in Babylon or shortly after returning. The tone is angry, to say the least. The psalm pleads with God to pay the Babylonians back for what they did to Jerusalem. It also expresses a longing for revenge against the Edomites who rejoiced as the Jews suffered. However, before you judge the writer too harshly, remember the horror the Babylonians unleashed. If we had lived through the same nightmare, these words might slip from our mouths. The psalmists were honest with God about the whole range of their emotions, including doubt, vengeful rage, and grief.

Psalms 144–150

The book of Psalms ends just as we would expect. The final seven songs focus on singing praises to our God. They call us to worship him at all times and with everything within us. Break out the instruments and shout his praise, the psalmist tells us. But he doesn't stop there. Psalm 148 calls on all of creation, from the highest heavens to the depths of the ocean, to join in the song. The Writings tell us how true believers act and react to the changing world around them. The last few psalms remind us that no matter what happens, we are to continually sing praises to our God. Nothing keeps this temporary world in its proper perspective quite like worshiping God, who sits on his throne. No problem ever looks quite as formidable after we spend time in the presence of the Lord.

Job

If God acted in a way that didn't appear to be good, would we still follow him? If he stopped answering prayer and stopped shielding us from the worst-case scenarios, would his praises fall from our lips? If the blessings dried up and life took a hard turn for the worse, what would happen to our faith?

These questions were more than theory for Job. Even though he loved God with a fervor unmatched in his day, he suffered in ways few people ever have. In one day Job lost everything. His family, his wealth, his health, his close relationship with the Lord — all of it disappeared in an instant. The finest man in all the earth found himself instead penniless and covered with painful boils. Grief swept over him as all ten of his children died when a storm destroyed the house where they were all together. All of this might have been bearable if the Lord had stood by his side. But suddenly Job felt alone. His prayers seemed to bounce back to the ground unheard. Everything around him screamed that God had turned his back on him.

Which brings us to the heart of the book of Job. This unhappy turn of events came about because Satan accused God of buying Job's love. In essence, the Devil told God the only reason Job (or anyone else) believed was because God blessed his life. Take away the blessings, Satan asserted, and Job and everyone else who claims to love God will curse him rather than sing his praises. The Devil is accusing God of buying us all off, of bribing us into serving him. The accusation hits us as well. It forces us to ask ourselves, *Why do I serve God?* Does God have to continually fill our lives with good things to keep us in his family? And will we continue to cling to him by faith when the circumstances in our lives shout that we are wasting our time?

JOB'S PLACE IN GOD'S STORY TIMELINE

Job may be the oldest book in the Bible. The events most likely took place long before Moses came down from Mount Sinai with the Law. Job probably lived around the same time as Abraham or one of the other patriarchs, or around eighteen hundred to two thousand years before Jesus. The book doesn't say who put this story into written form. Jewish tradition suggests Moses was the author, others say Job himself wrote his story down. Since the book itself doesn't say who wrote it, any guess is just that, a guess.

Job 1–6

The first two chapters set the stage by showing us a scene in heaven where Satan challenges God and attacks Job. This heavenly perspective allows us to understand the story in a way those living it can't. We know God hasn't turned against Job. Instead, we hear God praise his servant as the finest man on the planet. We also know Job's trials are a test instigated by the Devil himself. This inside knowledge allows us to make sense of what follows.

The rest of the book consists of a series of conversations between Job and the four men who visit him in his distress, Eliphaz, Bildad, Zophar, and later Elihu. They mean well, but the horror in front of them boggles their minds. Before any of them opens his mouth, the first three comforters sit with Job on a pile of ashes for seven days. During this time they survey the situation around them and weigh it against what they thought they knew about Job. All three reach the same conclusion: There must have been more to Job than meets the eye. All of them firmly believed God rewards the righteous and punishes the wicked. Since Job was obviously being punished, he must have harbored some dark, secret sins. Their theology wouldn't let them reach any other conclusion.

As you read Job's story, your preconceived notions about God will also be put to the test. Job's three friends aren't the only ones who assume right living will always be rewarded. The same idea lurks in the back of our minds. Deep down many of us believe God blesses the righteous and punishes the wicked. Therefore, if we want to be blessed, we should follow God and serve him. Those ideas are exactly what Satan accused God of doing. If we serve him only for the blessings, haven't we been bought off as well?

Job 7–14

Chapter 7 shows Job's anguish goes beyond the physical losses. His greatest fear is now a reality. That fear was not the death of his children or the loss of his wealth. Instead, he feared he would someday lose his intimacy with God. Now that has happened. As chapter 7 shows, he now feels God is tormenting him rather than giving him comfort. His words don't sound very faithful, unless you've experienced the same depths of suffering.

As Bildad speaks up, try to hear his words through Job's ears. Remember, Job isn't being punished. We know this, because we listened in on the conversation between God and Satan. Job now cries out like a man trying to make sense of a nightmare, and all he hears in response is, "How long will you go on like this? Your words are a blustering wind." Bildad doesn't offer hope or compassion. Instead, he wants to prove he is right and Job is wrong.

Notice as well how the intensity and anger in Job's comforters rise with each of their speeches. Zophar's first response in chapter 11 is much more cutting than Eliphaz's in chapters 4–5. He pulls off the gloves and goes after Job. You almost get the impression

Zophar derives some joy from Job's finally getting what he had coming. In fact, Zophar thinks God is holding back and Job should be punished even more. He tells Job, "Know this: God has even forgotten some of your sin" (Job 11:6, NIV). What a great friend to have.

Job 15–21

In spite of his anguish, Job doesn't curse God or abandon faith in him as a worthless cause. If anything, he pursues him with even greater urgency. Listen to 17:3: "You must defend my innocence, O God, since no one else will stand up for me." Satan thought God had bribed Job into trusting in him. Yet now, after Job has not only lost everything but also been accused of being a fraud, he won't let go of the Lord's hand. He pleads with God to stop tormenting him yet never stops believing. Not once does he pass off believing as the path of fools.

These chapters also show us how people of faith respond to difficulties. They don't put on a brave front and pretend the pain doesn't exist. Instead, they hurt, they cry out, they feel as though they can't hold on another moment, and yet they keep on believing.

Job 22–26

The third round of speeches is much shorter. Zophar is so disgusted he doesn't bother saying anything. Apparently he thinks Job is a lost cause. Job's response in chapter 24 moves away from idealized fantasies about life on this earth to its gritty reality. The wicked are not always punished. In fact, the rich oppress the poor and get away with it. They commit horrible acts and turn around and pervert justice. Why? Why doesn't God act? Why doesn't he do anything? Job's words sound like they could come from a twenty-first-century skeptic. He touches on the very issues that cause many people to reject Christianity. Yet if you listen, you hear something else. If the wicked don't get theirs in this world, there must be more than this life. The fact that justice doesn't rule in this world demands there must be a world to come.

Job 27–31

Job's final speech is the climax of the book. These chapters bring us face-to-face with faith and faithfulness and suffering. Chapter 28 is the centerpiece. Real wisdom, Job tells us, begins with the fear of the Lord. The word *fear* means fear, the same sort of knee-knocking terror Job feels. Yet what else can any rational person feel when he comes into the presence of a Sovereign God? Job shows us the real problem with his friends' theology is that it reduces God to a formula or the heavenly equivalent of an ATM. Punch in the right code, and blessing pours out. That isn't who God is at all.

Job 32–37

These chapters introduce a new character to the drama: Elihu. We don't know much about him. He is a young man who has watched the previous discussions in silence. He tries to find a middle ground by condemning both Job's friends and Job. Neither Job nor his comforters respond to Elihu.

Job 38–42

Finally God speaks. Job has cried out for answers, and now God is going to respond. But he doesn't explain himself. As you read, listen to the Lord's real message. What is he saying as he asks Job questions? If you were in Job's position, would God's words be enough? They were for Job.

Proverbs

God gave us the book of Proverbs to make us wise. The book does more than give us handy little sayings. It embodies the essence of a godly worldview. True wisdom begins with the fear of the Lord (Proverbs 1:7). This phrase speaks of a life that loves, worships, and obeys the Lord. To fear the Lord is to walk according to his Law and pattern our steps after his. Proverbs shows us how the fear of the Lord expresses itself in daily life. It builds on the Law but also expands on God's truth that is self-evident in creation. In short, this book guides us in applying to our lives all God has to say.

These proverbs show us how to live wise and godly lives. However, we need to be careful how we use them. They aren't meant to be taken as promises guaranteed by God. For example, Proverbs 22:6 says, "Train a child in the way he should go, and when he is old he will not turn from it" (NIV). Some see this verse as a guarantee from God that if parents do the right thing in teaching their children to love God, their children will never rebel against them or God. If this is a guarantee, the flipside goes something like this: If a child does go the wrong way, the parent must not have trained him right.

Is this true? Is every rebellious child the product of bad parenting? Of course not. Proverbs 22:6 tells us how wise parents raise their children, and how wise children respond. It also gives hope to those parents who suffer through the pain of a child's rebellion. Like the prodigal, someday their child may realize his parents did know what they were talking about, come to his senses, and come back to God.

This is but one example. Wisdom uses the proverbs wisely. We must be careful not to misapply them or stretch them beyond the clear teaching of the Bible as a whole. Instead, we must learn from them and pattern our lives after them. Wisdom begins with the fear of the Lord. That's where we need to start as well.

Proverbs 1–4

What is this fear of the Lord that is the beginning of wisdom? And does this mean we are supposed to be afraid of God? The word translated *fear* can also mean "terror." We see the word in action whenever someone came face-to-face with God. Isaiah cried out in terror, saying, "Woe is me," when he saw God in his temple. And John fell on his face like a dead man when he saw the risen Christ in a vision. Obviously, both men felt more than reverence and respect. Their knees went limp, and terror swept over them. Does that mean we should be afraid of God? In a word, yes. However, that isn't the only emotion we feel when we draw near to God. First John 4:18 says God's perfect love drives out all fear, allowing us to draw near to God as he draws near to us.

Proverbs 5–9

These five chapters continue Solomon's instructions to his children. Three times he addresses sexual immorality, in chapters 5, 6, and 7. His words not only expand on the seventh commandment, they show the wisdom behind it. God isn't trying to limit his children's fun when he prohibits sex outside of marriage. As these chapters show, immorality destroys the lives of those who engage in it. Yet keeping oneself pure requires more than simply saying no to sin. Temptation comes looking for us. It hunts us down and makes an offer hard to refuse. Yet it only leads to death. Although our bodies may not physically cease to exist, death and destruction still come with sexual immorality. Our culture mocks these words, yet post-sexual-revolution America shows how true they are.

The best defense against temptation is to wisely choose something greater. Verses 5:15-20 describe the way a husband and wife should look at one another. As Solomon says, "Rejoice in the wife of your youth. . . . May you always be captivated by her love." His words show how avoiding temptation is a matter of settling for more, not less. The joy that comes from a strong, healthy marriage far outweighs the short-term thrill of sexual escapades.

Proverbs 10–12

Chapters 10–29 present a series of proverbs and wise sayings. Most are not tied together in any way. Instead, each statement stands alone. Together they show us how to live wisely in a fallen world. Also, keep in mind the intent of each of the phrases. Some can be taken out of context and used in a way God did not intend. For example, 10:22 says, "The blessing of the LORD makes a person rich, and he adds no sorrow with it." Does this mean God wants to make all of us wealthy and exclude us from the suffering that besets the rest of the world? If it did, the book of Job would have to be taken out of the Bible. Instead, we need to understand this verse in light of the rest of the Bible. The blessings of God are the riches of the righteous. Ephesians 1 describes the incredible wealth we have in Christ, yet none of it has anything to do with something as temporary and insignificant as money.

Proverbs 13–16

Letting godly wisdom guide our lives changes all of our relationships. It transforms the way we raise our children and interact with the people around us. We even see ourselves differently while our goals in life are altered. We often wonder how we are supposed to live this Christian life in our day-to-day world. Here are some answers.

Proverbs 17–21

Wisdom not only touches our relationships with others, it shapes our understanding of God. In these chapters we find the Lord searches not just our actions, but our hearts as well. His searchlight penetrates the inner recesses of our souls, exposing every hidden motive. He is more pleased when we do what is just than when we offer him sacrifices. God is also actively involved in what goes on in this world. The heart of the king is in God's hand, which means the Lord can turn the hearts of even the mightiest rulers to do what he wants. Remember the words of Psalm 136. The Lord's faithful love endures forever. In Proverbs we see some of the ways he reveals this love to us.

Proverbs 22–26

Hebrews 13:5-6 tells us,

"Keep your lives free from the love of money and be content with what you have, because God has said,

> 'Never will I leave you;
>   never will I forsake you.'

So we say with confidence,

> 'The Lord is my helper; I will not be afraid.
>   What can man do to me?'" (NIV)

Proverbs 22–26 show contentment in action. You will discover ways to guard your heart against the lure of this world and be satisfied with what you have.

Proverbs 27–31

Agur, son of Jakeh, penned chapter 30. We don't know much about Agur beyond this chapter. He draws lessons from nature to show us how to live wisely. Chapter 31 was penned by King Lemuel, who was not a king over Israel or Judah. The chapter focuses on how a wise wife conducts herself. He describes a type of beauty that goes beyond physical features. Charm is deceptive and beauty doesn't last, but godliness will be greatly praised.

Ruth

Ruth is the first of four books that deal with some of the most basic questions we face as we try to walk with Christ by faith. It explores love and loyalty in the face of difficulties. In Ruth we find an unexpected romance between Ruth and Boaz. Ruth is a widow from Moab. Her late husband, who was from the tribe of Judah, died in Moab. But Ruth remains loyal to her widowed mother-in-law, and the two travel back to Judah. There they meet Boaz, who is older than Ruth and related to her dead husband. According to the Law of Moses, Boaz could marry Ruth and preserve her dead husband's name. However, there is another man who is closer in line. The book of Ruth traces the power of love and the lengths to which Boaz goes to make Ruth his own. Ruth and Song of Solomon come back-to-back because both books revolve around love stories. The book itself was probably written during the time of King David.

Song of Solomon

The Song of Solomon explores romantic love. Some of the poem's images sound odd today (few modern girls want their hair compared to a flock of goats), while others (the garden, the palm tree) remain as racy as ever. The speeches going back and forth between the two lovers explore the joys of physical love within marriage so explicitly that some commentators throughout history have seen the book as an allegory of God's love for his people. However, the book plainly expresses the range of emotions felt between human lovers. Consider 8:6-7 for wedding vows, or many sections for honeymoon reading. Some of the expressions are out-of-date, but you'll get the idea.

Traditionally, the book has been attributed to Solomon and was likely written early in his reign, around 960 BC.

Ecclesiastes

Ecclesiastes takes a long, hard look at life and asks the question with which philosophers have wrestled since the beginning of time: What's the point of life, anyway? Solomon wrote this book late in life as he searched for meaning and significance behind everything he'd accomplished. What he found is either incredibly depressing or enlightening. He discovered everything he had ever done really didn't matter. His wealth, his power, his building projects, the women—none of it meant anything. Life spins around like an endless cycle that soon sucks people down into death.

To find out what he finally concludes, read this book with an observant eye. Listen closely to what he says and what he doesn't. Try to place yourself in the flow of emotion. Immerse yourself in the book, and look at your own life as Solomon looks at his. What will you find there?

This book is perhaps the most modern (or postmodern) book in the Bible. We live in a time when people wonder if anything really matters. So why keep trying? Our culture can't give a credible answer. The best it can do is tell us life matters when we choose to make it matter. If that answer strikes you as lacking, it should. Solomon gave a much more credible answer 930 years before the birth of Christ. Look at his answer in light of Christ's cross.

Lamentations

The prophet Jeremiah penned Lamentations as the Babylonians destroyed Jerusalem (597–586 BC). The book consists of five poems of mourning lamenting the horrible tragedy brought about by the people's sins. Although the book is grouped with the other Major Prophets in English Bibles, it stands apart from Isaiah and the others. It doesn't warn of impending doom. Instead, it looks at what has already happened in light of God's Word. The first four chapters are acrostic poems in which each line begins with successive letters of the Hebrew alphabet.

The five poems of Lamentations do more than mourn Judah's devastating loss. They explain why this tragedy has struck. The first poem, chapter 1, explains how the misery Jerusalem is suffering is God's judgment for hundreds of years of sin. Lamentations 2 calls the people back to God in prayer. Chapter 3 is the high point. In the midst of this poem of sorrow comes a timeless statement of hope:

> I remember my affliction and my wandering,
>> the bitterness and the gall.
>
> I well remember them,
>> and my soul is downcast within me.
>
> Yet this I call to mind
>> and therefore I have hope:
>
> Because of the Lord's great love we are not consumed,
>> for his compassions never fail.
>
> They are new every morning;
>> great is your faithfulness.
>
> I say to myself, "The Lord is my portion;
>> therefore I will wait for him."
>
> (Lamentations 3:19–24, NIV)

The fourth poem of Lamentations paints a vivid picture of the horrors of the fall of Jerusalem and blames this judgment on the corrupt prophets and priests. Finally, chapter 5 recaps what has happened to the city and prays that God will restore his people.

The Writings address the question of how ordinary people lived out their faith in their day-to-day lives, especially in hard times. Lamentations is the classic example of what the Writings are about. The mood is mournful, yet hope prevails. It reveals faith in action.

Esther

Esther is the first of the three books that tell the stories of men and women with the courage and faith to take unpopular stands for God. Her story takes place around 470 BC, or more than 115 years after the fall of Jerusalem and nearly forty years after the Jews are allowed to return home. Yet many Jews didn't return, including Esther's family. They stayed where they'd been resettled and established homes. For the most part, these Jews enjoyed a fairly normal existence. The Babylonian Empire fell in 539 BC to the Persian King Cyrus, who showed particular favor to the Jews. He was the one who allowed them to return to their homes and rebuild the temple.

By the time Esther comes along, the Jewish people are treated as a normal part of the population. They live as merchants and farmers, and for the most part they are allowed to live as a distinct minority. However, then as now, there were those who hated the Jews because of their devotion to one God. The efforts of a man named Haman to finally do away with the Jews once and for all is the centerpiece of this story. Only one person stands between the Jews and destruction, the unlikely queen, a young Jewish woman who up until this time has kept her nationality a secret—Esther.

In addition to Esther, this book has some great characters. Working behind the scenes is Esther's cousin Mordecai, who raised her after her parents died. He is a fearless man who never craved credit for anything he did. The frustrated prime minister, Haman, hates Mordecai. When Mordecai refuses to bow down before Haman, Haman hatches his plot to exact his revenge upon the entire Jewish people. Then there is Esther herself. She risks her own life to save her people.

The story of Esther is the story of God's sovereignty, even though he is never mentioned by name. Even so, he fills every page. You can see his hand moving events and people to accomplish his will. Reading this story helps us become aware of God working in our own lives as well. The Jews continue to celebrate the events of this book in their annual Feast of Purim.

Daniel

Daniel's inclusion in the Writings rather than the Prophets strikes most of us as odd. Yet the reason should become clear as you read it. Isaiah, Jeremiah, and the others predicted future events, but those events always revolve around God's coming judgment and promises of restoration. Daniel focuses on coming kingdoms and more specific historical events. The other prophets build around three themes: sin, punishment, and restoration. Daniel does not. Also, the other prophets speak in the name of the Lord. Some variation of the phrase "This is what the Sovereign LORD says" can be found in almost all of them. Even when the phrase isn't stated directly, it is implied. But not in Daniel. Daniel's prophetic section revolves around dreams and their interpretation. This book contains prophetic predictions, but it is nothing like the other prophets, so it appears in the Writings, not the Prophets.

The events of the book cover a period from 605 to 535 BC. Most scholars believe Daniel finished recording his visions and his story toward the end of his life, around 535 BC.

Daniel 1–6

Reading Daniel is almost like reading two separate books. The first half tells a series of stories about trials of faith during the Exile. Daniel and three of his friends, Hananiah, Mishael, and Azariah, are carried off by the Babylonian armies from their homes in Jerusalem when they are "young men," which probably means their early teens (if that old). The Babylonians nab them because they are among Judah's best and brightest. Once they arrive in their new home, the four receive new names and go into training for service in the king's courts. We are more familiar with Daniel's three friends by these new names, Shadrach, Meshach, and Abednego.

But life in Babylon isn't easy for these four who are determined to serve the Lord. Their faith is tested time and again. Daniel records six specific tests that span the rest of his and his friends' lives in Babylon. The stakes are always high. More than once they risk death rather than disobey their God or worship anyone but him. The stories of Shadrach, Meshach, and Abednego in the fiery furnace and Daniel in the lion's den are two of the first stories children hear about God. These tales show us how to live in a land that is hostile to our faith. They also demonstrate God's faithfulness in our deepest trials.

Daniel 7–12

All of the visions of Daniel 7–12 involve the rise and fall of future kingdoms. The first dream, chapter 7, involves four kingdoms, most likely Babylon, Persia, Greece, and Rome. The second dream, chapter 8, focuses on the transition between the second two kingdoms, Persia and Greece. The large horn on the head of the ram that represents Greece refers to Alexander the Great. He will extend his kingdom across the known world, yet die at the peak of his power. After his death the kingdom will be divided into four districts. Chapter 10 takes us to these four districts. The king of one of the districts will later persecute the Jews and defile the rebuilt temple in Jerusalem, going so far as to sacrifice a pig on the altar. These events will be fulfilled during the time of the Maccabees, in the four-hundred-year interim between the Old and New Testaments. Chapters 10–12 refer to future events that haven't yet taken place. In some ways they are similar to the book of Revelation. Interpreting these six chapters is difficult, to say the least. Their tone is apocalyptic and filled with symbolism that the book doesn't explain.

Ezra

Like the books of Esther and Daniel, Ezra tells the story of a man who stands up for God in a moment of crisis. Ezra was a priest and an expert in the Law. He grew up with the exiles in Babylon. During the reign of the Persian King Artaxerxes (465–425 BC), Ezra and a large group of Jews returned to their ancestral homeland. Although the temple had been rebuilt and worship of the Lord restored, the situation into which Ezra walked caused him to cry out to the Lord in shame. The Jews living in Judah were intermarrying with the nations around them. Ezra found this disturbing not because he was racist. Far from it. Instead, he found this trend alarming because he knew his people's history. Intermarriage with pagan nations meant adopting their religious practices. If left unchecked, the pattern of spiritual adultery that led to the Exile would start repeating itself. Ezra could not let that happen.

Ezra's devotion to the Law paved the way for a new group of leaders in Judea who guided the people in their understanding of God's Word. With time this group also lost their way. They didn't fall into idolatry, not in the traditional sense. Instead, they made the Law into a type of idol and reduced obedience to a formula rather than an act of faith. Four hundred years after Ezra, these people who claimed him as their founder (even though they missed his point entirely) made Jesus' life miserable. We know them as the Pharisees.

Ezra 1–6

The first six chapters of Ezra tell the story of the decree by Cyrus that allowed the Jews to return to their homes and rebuild the temple. Most of these events took place before Ezra was born.

He also places a great deal of emphasis on genealogies. We find these boring, yet they show us God's faithfulness to his people generation after generation.

As you read today, pay close attention to 4:1-5. The people who ask if they can help build the temple are the Samaritans, the descendants of the people the Assyrians used to repopulate the territories of the northern ten tribes. This passage can help illuminate the hostility between Jews and Samaritans in the New Testament.

Ezra 7–10

The central character of the book finally arrives in chapter 7. Compare the way he confronts the people with their sin in chapter 9 — and especially their response — with the reception Jeremiah and the other prophets received. What makes the difference? Also, the story doesn't end in Ezra 10. It continues in the book of Nehemiah.

Nehemiah

The prophets who spoke to Israel and Judah before their exile didn't come with just a message of doom. They promised God would bring the people home and give them a future that would outshine their past (Jeremiah 29:11). But nearly eighty years after Cyrus allowed the Jews to return home, these promises seemed like a cruel joke. The people had managed to rebuild the temple and begin worshiping the Lord as the Law requires, but the city still bore the scars of Nebuchadnezzar's attacks 140 years earlier. The city's walls lay in ruins, and the gates were missing from the few portions that stood intact. In the ancient world, a city without walls wasn't much of a city. Even though the Jews were home, they still felt like refugees. Fear ruled the day, while people wondered if God had forgotten them.

Nehemiah's story was put into written form around 420 BC. It demonstrates the power of prayer and God's faithfulness to those courageous enough to step out in faith.

Nehemiah 1–7

As cupbearer to the Persian King Artaxerxes, Nehemiah does more than pick out fine wines for the king. In the ancient world, a regime change was as close as finding a way to eliminate the king. Poison was a popular weapon of choice. Therefore Nehemiah serves as one of the king's last lines of defense. His character has to be impeccable. The king literally puts his life in Nehemiah's hands.

Nehemiah 8–13

After the walls are completed, a new task confronts Nehemiah: rebuilding the people's lives. He uses wood and stone and mortar to rebuild the walls, but he uses the Word of God to rebuild the people. The latter half of the book tells how the people respond and of the revival that breaks out. Nothing like this has ever taken place in their history. The people take responsibility for their sins and the sins of their ancestors that incurred God's wrath. Not only do they confess their sins, they sign their names to a covenant to obey the Lord. Then they go out and change their behavior. The land is filled with changed lives, all under Nehemiah's leadership. As you read, pay close attention to the way Nehemiah always deflects praise from himself to God. No wonder God used him in such a mighty way.

First and Second Chronicles

First and Second Chronicles are more than a retelling of Israel's story. The books show us how to view history. Rather than seeing the past as an end in itself, we need to have an eye toward the future and the hope God gives. Israel's story is filled with missed opportunities and disobedience that led to catastrophe. But that isn't the end of the story. All along the way God held out the hope of restoration and the fulfillment of his promises. Long ago he promised to bless all the nations through Abraham's descendants. Reading the Former Prophets, Joshua through Kings, we saw how Israel did everything in her power to keep this from happening. The end result was seventy years in exile and the loss of the ten northern tribes.

Chronicles opens our eyes to the same events from a completely different perspective. In spite of Israel's failures, in spite of her headlong attempts to run away from God, his plan hasn't changed. The Lord's covenant with Abraham still stands. Through these books, God tells the people who think their best days are far behind them to get up, stop feeling sorry for themselves, and go forward with God. The judgment of the past is now in the past. Learn from it. Turn away from sin. And move forward.

Jewish tradition holds that Ezra wrote Chronicles, although the books themselves never mention an author. Whether or not Ezra wrote them, the books date from the same period as Ezra–Nehemiah, around 430 BC, or around a hundred years after the first of the Jews returned to the Promised Land from Babylon.

1 Chronicles 1–9

Chronicles doesn't exactly start off with a bang. The genealogies don't make for compelling reading. However, they played a key role for the original audience. The Jews who first read these books felt adrift both physically and spiritually. The genealogies gave them roots. "With these roots God's people knew who they were and how they were to live. They may have felt like the most insignificant of peoples (a small, backwater country in the great Persian Empire), but the genealogies served to remind them that they were not only a people with a rich history, but that their history was God's history."[1] Don't worry if you can't find any life-changing truths in nine chapters of "Adam was the father of Seth." Just look at them as a testimony to God's faithfulness, and remember, he hasn't changed.

1 Chronicles 10–15

The chronicler wrote to remind the downtrodden Jews who have returned from exile of their heritage in the Lord God. They aren't just descendants of Abraham, Isaac, and Jacob. They are God's chosen people. You begin to see this emphasis as the story moves to David. God appoints David king over all of Israel. Even before he comes to power, during the time Saul chases him around and tries to kill him, people from all twelve tribes stand and fight with him. The chronicler also tells us of the exploits of David's mighty men, the Three and the Thirty, who win great battles for their king. These men are heroes who prevail against impossible odds. These stories should have been a great encouragement to the Jews of 430 BC, who tremble in fear behind Jerusalem's broken walls. God doesn't need a huge army to give his people victory. He has fought Israel's battles in the past, and he will continue to do so.

Chapters 13 and 15 also emphasize a topic that plays a major role in both 1 and 2 Chronicles: worship. God has created Israel to be more than another geopolitical state. He calls the people to know and worship him. They fully express their identity as his chosen people as they gather together before him and sing his praises. The centerpiece of the kingdom is therefore not the king, but the tabernacle and temple that house the ark of the covenant.

1 Chronicles 16–20

These chapters retell Israel's golden age. God gives David victory over all his enemies. As a result, Israel's borders and influence extend all the way to the Euphrates River, just as God promised Abraham and Moses. In the midst of it all, God makes a new promise. He tells David he will have a dynasty that will last forever. One of David's descendants will always sit on Israel's throne. That is why Jesus had to be a descendant of David. He is the ultimate fulfillment of this promise. Jesus is the Messiah, the Anointed One for whom the Jews of 430 BC longed.

1 Chronicles 21–29

Chapters 21–29 all focus on David's role in building the temple. He devotes the latter years of his reign to assembling the raw materials his son will need to build the building itself. He amasses tons of gold and silver, along with bronze and iron. God won't let David build the temple himself, but that doesn't stop David from doing everything in his power to insure this will be the greatest building ever built. He even draws up the plans and gives them to his son. This emphasis shows that David's greatest legacy is not his military victories, but his passion for the Lord.

2 Chronicles 1–7

Four hundred years of history are squeezed into 2 Chronicles' thirty-six chapters. With so little space and so much to cover, you would expect the chronicler to focus on the major battles and other turning points. Most historians take this approach. But the chronicler is no ordinary historian. He calls the people to make the Lord the centerpiece of their lives. They are to serve and obey him above everything else. And they are to worship him. That's why they exist.

For this reason, you shouldn't be surprised to find seven chapters devoted solely to the building and dedication of the temple. This building is more than a structure of wood, stone, and precious metals. After Solomon places the ark of the covenant within the Holy of Holies, the glory of God fills the place in the form of a thick cloud. The parallel between this event and the dedication of the tabernacle in the wilderness is intentional. Israel is not just God's chosen people. She is the unique people among whom God dwells. Now Israel is to make him known to the world. From this moment forward, her fate as a nation and her fidelity to the Lord are inseparably linked. The rest of the story is more than a tale of political and strategic risings and falls. Instead, it is a story of the people's faithfulness or unfaithfulness to the Lord.

2 Chronicles 8–12

At this point in the story, 1 Kings focused most of its attention on the northern tribes who split away. Chronicles fills in the details from the south. Here we learn Rehoboam, Solomon's heir to the throne, initially listens to the Lord. For three years he leads the people to serve the Lord. People from the northern kingdom who can't stomach Jeroboam's false gods move to Judah to worship and serve the Lord. But once Rehoboam has a firm grip on the throne, he turns from God and leads the people into idolatry. As a result, Pharoah Shishak of Egypt attacks and carries away the wealth Solomon accumulated. (Some historians believe Shishak carried off the ark of the covenant as well, although few scholars accept this theory as true.)

2 Chronicles 13–17

King Abijah stands in sharp contrast to his father, Rehoboam. Abijah trusts in the Lord alone. Even when he is outnumbered two to one on the battlefield against the seasoned armies of Jeroboam, he relies on the Lord rather than on his own strength, and God gives him the victory. As you read chapter 13, you will be reminded that every battle is essentially a contest of deities. The question of the day isn't which god is stronger, but which god is real. You can hear this in Abijah's voice as he compares the one true God to the golden calves the northern tribes worship.

2 Chronicles 18–23

Deuteronomy 17:18-19 commands the king to write out a copy of the Law for himself. Then he is to study it every day "so that he may learn to revere the LORD his God and follow carefully all the words of this law and these decrees" (Deuteronomy 17:19, NIV). Jehoshaphat takes this law one step further. In 2 Chronicles 19, he travels throughout the country encouraging the people to return to the Lord. When he appoints judges, he gives them strict instructions to carry out their duties in a way that will please the Lord, regardless of what people think. The Law of God becomes the central focus of Jehoshaphat's reign.

Chapters 21–23 show how quickly the efforts of a godly man like Jehoshaphat can be undone. His son Jehoram follows the example of the Baal-worshiping northern kingdom rather than the example of his father. His death is gruesome, and he is buried with this epitaph: "No one was sorry when he died" (2 Chronicles 21:20). His son, Ahaziah, is no better and rules only one year. When he dies, the Queen Mother, Athaliah, takes over and tries to kill every legitimate heir to the throne. What will be the long-term consequences if she succeeds? How will her actions affect God's promise to David? God's response to Athaliah's action shows he won't allow anything to derail his plans. Once he speaks, his word will come to pass.

2 Chronicles 24–28

The constant pendulum swinging between faithfulness to the Lord and idolatry grows more pronounced in these five chapters. Joash is faithful through the beginning of his reign, but as he grows older, he turns from the Lord. When the prophet Zechariah confronts him, Joash orders the prophet's execution. Jesus mentions Zechariah's death in Matthew 23:29-35.

Joash's son, Amaziah, moves even further away from the Lord, and God destroys him for it. The next king, Uzziah, doesn't worship idols, but he also fails to show respect for the Lord or his Law. Isaiah begins his ministry during Uzziah's reign. King Ahaz takes idolatry to a new low. He closes the temple, destroys many of the utensils used in the Lord's worship, and enshrines the gods of Syria. How much lower can the kingdom go?

2 Chronicles 29–36

The key difference between Chronicles and Kings is found in the way each concludes its telling of Israel's history. Kings ended with judgment. Judah and Jerusalem were destroyed, their people carried off as captives to Babylon. In this way, Kings emphasizes the consequences of sin and urges the reader to turn back to God. Chronicles ends with Cyrus's decree allowing the Jews to return home. With this, God says his plan is still alive. His promises still stand. Now is the time to go forward with him. By ending on this note, the Old Testament leaves us asking, *What will God do next?* The answer will come four hundred years later in a barn in Bethlehem.

The Good News

Matthew, Mark,
Luke, John, Acts

AUTHORS

Each gospel bears the name of the man who wrote it. Luke wrote both his gospel and the book of Acts.

WHEN WERE THESE BOOKS WRITTEN?

None of the Gospels were written until more than twenty years after Jesus rose from the dead. Why the delay? Most believers fully expected Jesus to return at any moment. Writing out accounts of his life for future generations, therefore, didn't make much sense. Mark's gospel was probably written first, around the year 55. John's was the last, most likely written between the years 75 and 80. Matthew, Luke, and Acts were all probably written in that order sometime between 60 and 65.

WHAT ARE THEY ABOUT?

In a word—Jesus. But these books are about Jesus as God's final act to answer once and for all the two questions that echo through the Bible: Who is God, and how can sinful people live in any kind of relationship with a holy God? Since the human race would never be able to come close to finding the answers to these questions, God answered them himself by taking on flesh and coming to earth. As for who God is, John 1:18 says, "No one has ever seen God. But his only Son, who is himself God, is near to the Father's heart; he has told us about him." That last phrase is much stronger in the original language than it appears in English translations. It means to explain or reveal something fully. Jesus didn't just tell us about the Father, he came to make everything we needed to know about him fully known through both his words and his actions. As he told his disciples, "Anyone who has seen me has seen the Father!" (John 14:9).

Jesus gave the final answer to the second question as well. Both the Law and the history of ancient Israel make it clear that no human being can live up to what a holy God requires. The problem isn't that God's standards are too high, but that human beings, creatures made in God's image, have so sold ourselves to sin that we are no longer capable of doing what God made us to do. How then can anyone be made right with God? Jesus is the answer. Romans 8:3-4 puts it this way:

The law of Moses could not save us, because of our sinful nature. But God put into effect a different plan to save us. He sent his own Son in a human body like ours, except that ours are sinful. God destroyed sin's control over us by giving his Son as a sacrifice for our sins. He did this so that the requirement of the law would be fully accomplished for us who no longer follow our sinful nature but instead follow the Spirit.

That is why Jesus came. That is the good news.

Before you dive into the Gospels and the rest of the New Testament, you need to understand a few key truths regarding why Jesus came and what he did. First, God's sending his Son was not a new course of action, but the next logical step in all he did to reveal himself in the Old Testament. All that came before in God's story led to a manger in Bethlehem and, ultimately, to the cross. Second, everything you will read in the New Testament has its roots in the Old. The ideas here are not new. God didn't change his plan of salvation. Faith was the heart of the Law and the one thing God sought in all those who would come to him. If you need proof, go back and reread Deuteronomy 6. Finally, to understand the New Testament, you need to read it in light of the Old. The Gospels and letters flow out of the Law, the Prophets, and the Writings. To fully appreciate and understand part two of God's story, you need to read part one.

Matthew

Plot: Jesus the Messiah has come, just as the Law, the Prophets, and the Writings promised. He comes to establish the kingdom of God on earth, but that kingdom is not what the Jews expected. Matthew wrote for a predominantly Jewish audience.

Key characters: Joseph, Jesus, the twelve disciples, the Pharisees and Sadducees

Turning point in the story: Matthew 16

Mark

Plot: Jesus is Savior and the King of kings. His authority extends over every other authority, both in heaven and on earth. Mark wrote to fellow believers in Rome who desperately needed to hear this truth.

Key characters: John the Baptist, Jesus, the twelve disciples

Turning point in the story: Mark 8:27-30

Luke

Plot: Luke is the gospel for the outcasts. As the only Gentile God used to write books of the Bible, he knew what it felt like to be on the outside looking in. Luke wrote to a Gentile audience, emphasizing Jesus' humanity and his identification with those the rest of the world rejected.

Key characters: Zechariah, Elizabeth, Mary, Jesus, the twelve disciples, Pilate, Herod, the thief on the cross

Turning point in the story: Luke 9

John

Plot: "These are written so that you may believe that Jesus is the Messiah, the Son of God, and that by believing in him you will have life" (John 20:31). That is the point of the fourth gospel.

Key characters: The usual suspects along with Nicodemus, Lazarus, Martha, Mary, Pilate

Turning point in the story: John 6:60-71

Acts

Plot: Acts is volume two of Luke's account. The good news came with Jesus. In Acts we see how it spread across the known world, fulfilling the promise God made to Abraham when he said all the nations would be blessed through him.

Key characters: Peter, John, Cornelius, Barnabas, Paul, Silas

Turning point in the story: Acts 9

Matthew

As a Jew, Matthew grew up hearing the stories of Abraham and Moses and David. Like any good Jewish child growing up in Judea in the first century, he learned the Law and all God required of his chosen people. But he didn't stick with the Law after he grew up. In first-century Judea, any Jew who willingly worked with the Romans was a traitor to his people. Tax collectors were even worse. Not only did they work for Rome, they also earned their livings by overcharging and keeping the difference for themselves. Matthew walked away from this lucrative life the day Jesus called him to be his disciple (Matthew 9:9).

When Matthew wrote the gospel that bears his name, he did so with an understanding of the Law, Prophets, and Writings that was transformed by the grace he found in Jesus. As a Jew, Matthew understood Jesus' life and ministry in light of God's promises to Israel through the prophets concerning the coming Messiah. This is why Matthew continually refers to the Old Testament to show how Jesus fulfilled what came before. When the Jews spoke of a coming Savior, they longed for a king who would take the throne of their greatest king, David. Matthew shows the power and authority Jesus possessed as King, but he also explains how the kingdom of God is more than a political entity. In Jesus the kingdom of heaven came down to earth, but not in the ways the Jews expected. The ultimate fulfillment of this part of God's promises awaits Jesus' return. Then he will take his place on the throne of David and rule over every nation. Until then he reigns as a King within the hearts of his followers. We first come to understand this dual nature of the kingdom of God through Matthew.

Matthew 1–2

Matthew traces Jesus' lineage through Abraham and David to remind us of the covenants God made with Israel through these men, covenants that find their ultimate fulfillment in Jesus. God's covenant with Abraham promised that the entire world would be blessed through Abraham's descendants (Genesis 12:1-3; 15:1-7; 17:1-8). The Lord promised David a dynasty that would last forever (2 Samuel 7:8-16). Not only would one of his descendants always sit on Israel's throne, but God vowed to love this future eternal King with an unfailing love that would also extend to his people. These two covenants come together in Jesus.

The Gospels aren't biographies. Matthew gives few details in the first two chapters concerning Jesus' birth and early childhood. The details he includes—the virgin birth, the visit of the Magi, the escape to Egypt, Jesus' family settling in Nazareth—are all included because each fulfills a specific prophecy in the Old Testament.

Matthew 3–4

To understand the ministry of John the Baptist, read Isaiah 40:3-5 and Malachi 3:1; 4:5-6. John was Elijah, not in the sense that he was the ancient prophet reincarnated, but rather a prophet who came with Elijah's spirit and power. You will appreciate what this means much better by reading the life of Elijah in 1 Kings 17–2 Kings 2. If you read only one part of his story, be sure to make it 1 Kings 18. John the Baptist comes with the same kind of fearlessness, standing up to the political and religious establishment regardless of the cost.

As you read chapters 3–4, consider why Jesus asks John to baptize him even though Jesus doesn't have any sins to confess.

Also, note how Jesus goes straight from John to be tempted by Satan. He goes from such a tremendous spiritual high where his Father spoke from heaven, to the lowest of lows where he is attacked by the Devil in his weakest moment. If this happened to Jesus, should we be surprised when we go through similar experiences? Also, pay close attention to how Jesus defeats Satan. Because Jesus is fully God, he could speak a word and destroy the Devil once and for all. Why doesn't he?

Matthew 5–7

These chapters are the Sermon on the Mount, the first of five blocks of Jesus' teaching in this book. Notice how Jesus refers to the Old Testament Law. He didn't come to abolish it, but to fulfill it. This doesn't lower the standard of behavior required of his followers. In fact, he raises the bar even higher. However, you can't keep Christ's commands mechanically through outward actions alone. To do the things found in these three chapters, you must first have God change your heart.

In the middle of this message, Jesus says, "Unless you obey God better than the teachers of religious law and the Pharisees do, you can't enter the Kingdom of Heaven at all!" (5:20). The Pharisees are the largest and most influential group of Jewish religious leaders at this time. The name *Pharisees* means "separated ones." It may mean they separate themselves from the common people or separate themselves to the study and interpretation of the Law. Both apply. While the priests see the temple sacrifices as the focus of the faith, the Pharisees emphasize personal obedience to the rest of the Law. They call their teachers *rabbi* and center their religious practice on the synagogue rather than the temple. Jesus' followers call him rabbi, and he agrees with many of the Pharisees' views. Like them, he emphasizes obeying God in daily life and teaches that God will raise his people from the dead at the end of this age.

However, the Pharisees have accumulated a vast body of oral traditions and interpretation of the Law. They treat these traditions as equal to the Law itself. They have interpretations for everything from how much to tithe of one's spices to the exact distance one can travel on the Sabbath before the journey constitutes work and violates the Law. In Jesus' view, this oral law burdens people and distracts them from the essentials of true obedience. True obedience, for Jesus, involves things like purging rage and lust from one's attitudes and loving one's enemies. That kind of obedience can't be achieved with a mechanical checklist system of dos and don'ts. It requires a total transformation of the mind and heart. Jesus claims the authority to throw out the Pharisees' interpretations of the Law in favor of his own. For this they oppose him bitterly.

Matthew 8–9

After the disciples watch Jesus calm the storm, they are in awe. Matthew uses a Greek word (translated "astonished" in The Message) that conveys the idea of both wonder and terror. In fact, Mark and Luke both include the most common word for fear in their accounts. The disciples are more than surprised, more than awed, more than afraid. They find themselves in a tiny boat with someone far greater, and therefore more terrifying, than the storm that causes them to scream like children. As Jesus goes back to sleep, they mutter, "Who is this?" Before you pass over their reaction too quickly, put yourself in their place. How comfortable would you feel around someone who could command the strongest winds to be quiet and be obeyed?

Chapter 9 begins with another miracle and another surprising reaction. The Pharisees feel neither awe nor wonder. Instead, Jesus' miracles make them mad. Why? Fear sweeps through the crowd as Jesus heals a paralyzed man, but the Pharisees slink off, their faces red and their ears burning. Here we see the first inkling of the hatred that would later lead them to demand Jesus' execution.

Matthew 10–11

Chapter 10 is the second major teaching Jesus delivers in the book of Matthew. Unlike the Sermon on the Mount (chapters 5–7), Jesus doesn't speak these words to a large crowd. Instead, in chapter 10 he addresses the twelve disciples as they prepare to take the good news about Jesus to all of Israel. Most of the chapter focuses on the opposition his disciples will face as they proclaim Jesus to the world. Note how Jesus tells them to respond to these attacks. He tells them not to be afraid. Suffering throws open the doors for the gospel to spread. History has proven these words to be true. An early Christian named Tertullian said, "The blood of the martyrs is the seed of the church." The more the world tries to squash the good news about Jesus, the more it spreads. Instead of shrinking back from persecution, true followers of Christ should embrace it.

Matthew 12–13

Jesus affirms the historical accuracy of the Old Testament by comparing himself to Jonah. Just as Jonah was in the belly of the great fish for three days, Jesus will be in the heart of the earth for three days. The crowd might have scratched their heads wondering what he meant, but we know Jesus was referring to the fact that he would be in the grave for three days before rising from the dead.

Chapter 13 is Jesus' third major sermon in this book. It also marks the first appearance of parables. Parables are stories with a spiritual message. The messages of these seven parables all revolve around the kingdom of heaven. The first will probably be the most familiar, the story of the farmer scattering seed. As you read, pay close attention to what the parable says about the role of difficulties in the lives of believers.

Matthew 14–15

Jesus feeds huge crowds with a very small amount of food on two different occasions. Notice how these stories are similar and different in their details. What point is Jesus trying to get across to his disciples through these two episodes? He never does miracles just for kicks. They always play a part in his greater mission and purpose. How do these two miracles fit into that purpose?

As you read about other miracles, put yourself in the place of the people who experienced them firsthand. Specifically, try to read the story of Jesus walking on water from the standpoint of those in the boat. Put yourself there. Would you get out of the boat? What makes Peter start to sink? Have you ever experienced anything like this where you took a big leap of faith with God, only to find yourself drowning in doubt later?

Matthew 16–17

Jesus first mentions the cross and his purpose for coming to earth in chapter 16. He makes it clear that he came to suffer and die. Yet in chapter 17 he gives three of the disciples a glimpse of who he really is. On top of a mountain during a private prayer retreat, Jesus pulls back his humanity and reveals his glory as God. Try to put yourself in the place of Peter, James, and John. How could you reconcile Jesus' talk of dying a horrible death with the glory you saw on the mountain? These two ideas—God made flesh, God dying on a cross—cannot go together in their minds. Yet this mystery, these two contradictory ideas, explains the life of Christ. Moses was the giver of the Law, and Elijah was the great prophet who didn't die but was taken directly to heaven. Here on this mountain, the Law and the Prophets confirm what the disciples already understand about Jesus.

Jesus addresses the Sadducees for the first time in chapter 16. They are a smaller group of religious leaders than the Pharisees. Most are wealthy aristocrats, while most Pharisees are common people. The Sadducees recognize only the first five books of the Old Testament as the authoritative Word of God. They don't believe in the resurrection of the dead or life after death. Nor do they believe in angels or demons. The high priests, who control the temple, are Sadducees.

Matthew 18

This chapter takes you through Jesus' fourth major sermon in the book of Matthew. Pay close attention to what it says about the life of a disciple. Notice how we are to deal with temptation and sin. We also have responsibilities to one another. If we see our brothers or sisters fall into sin, we must go to them. Gossip, or talk of how we knew they weren't serious, or standing by wringing our hands and doing nothing aren't options. If they sin against us, we must go to them. As we go to them, we must forgive them as Jesus has forgiven us.

Matthew 19–20

The events in these chapters take place on the road to Jerusalem. Large crowds follow Jesus, and he heals the sick. Matthew doesn't give any details regarding the miracles. He knows firsthand that miracles don't spawn great devotion to Christ. This same cheering crowd will soon be demanding Jesus' death.

Jesus' teaching in chapter 19 expands upon the Law of Moses, while chapter 20 sets the stage for the book's climax.

Matthew 21–22

In terms of his public ministry, these two chapters mark the high point of Jesus' popularity. When he rides into Jerusalem, the crowds honestly believe they are welcoming the Messiah who will deliver them from the Romans. They are partially correct, as Matthew points out. Jesus rides into the city on the back of a donkey to fulfill Zechariah 9:9. The Lord not only promised his King would come, he also told the Jews this King would bring peace to the nations and his realm would stretch to the ends of the earth. As the Jews spread their coats and palm branches in the streets and sing songs of praise to God and the King, they expect Jesus to establish a kingdom on earth immediately.

However, if they have been listening to everything Jesus has said about the kingdom, words Matthew carefully records, they will realize the kingdom of heaven is much more than a political reality. For Jesus to establish peace on the earth as Zechariah predicted, he would first have to defeat the source of all wars and suffering. And the only way he could defeat this greatest of all enemies mankind faces was by dying and rising again. The crowd's failure to grasp Jesus' message about the kingdom partially explains how quickly they turn against him. They feel betrayed, deceived. If Jesus isn't going to set them free from the Romans, who needs him? But we won't see this until chapter 26.

Matthew 23–25

These chapters contain Jesus' last major teaching block in this book. Jesus' words in all three chapters sound very much like those of one of the Old Testament prophets, for Jesus focuses on the coming Judgment. The tone is harsh and blunt, yet this is exactly what we should expect. With these final words, he aligns himself with all the prophets who came before him. Just as most of them suffered as a result of their message, Jesus will be no different. And that's the point. As in the parable of the landowner and the evil farmers in Matthew 21:33-46, the Son of God will suffer the same fate all of the Lord's previous messengers endured.

The events of which Jesus speaks in chapter 24 have, for all practical purposes, taken place. Most were fulfilled by AD 70 when the Romans destroyed Jerusalem and tore down the temple. This means that every generation of believers could be the last.

Matthew 26–27

Chapters 26–27 are two of the hardest chapters in the Bible to read. The betrayal, the denials, the lies told about Jesus to secure a death sentence are painful. Then there is chapter 27, with the beatings, the mockery, and finally Jesus' death as a criminal on a cross. Read these chapters slowly. Allow the details to soak in. Never forget Jesus did all of this because of our sin. He chose this fate. No one thrust it upon him. He wasn't a victim, not in the usual sense of the word. Jesus came to die the worst of all deaths. Where would we be without the rest of the story?

Matthew 28

Matthew ends triumphantly. Yet we also come away knowing this isn't the end of the story, but the beginning. The rest continues to be written today in the lives of Jesus' followers. As we go out with the gospel, he goes with us. The full impact of the life, death, and resurrection of Jesus won't be felt until the end of history.

Mark

The book of Mark was probably the first of the four Gospels to be written. Even though the author doesn't identify himself, the book has always been attributed to a man named John Mark. John Mark first appears in the Bible in Acts 12. Apparently the church in Jerusalem met for prayer in his mother's home. Later Paul and Barnabas took John Mark with them on their first missionary excursion (Acts 12:25).

At some point in time, John Mark began working with Peter. The two became very close, so close that Peter called him his son (1 Peter 5:13). Ancient writers refer to Mark as Peter's "disciple" and "interpreter." The latter phrase probably meant Mark put into writing the things Peter taught. And that's how John Mark came to write the book that bears his name. He put into words the stories of Jesus he heard Peter share time and time again. In fact, the gospel of Mark follows the general outline of the good news about Jesus that Peter gives in Acts 10:37-41. In a very real sense, then, the gospel according to Mark is Peter's telling of the story of Jesus' ministry.

The book of Mark targets a non-Jewish audience. We see this in the way Mark explains many of the Jewish customs and translates Aramaic words (the Jews in the first century spoke Aramaic). This first gospel to be penned probably was circulated around the city of Rome sometime between AD 55 and 65. By this time the apostles were scattered outside Judea, and most of the people who believed in Jesus were Gentiles. Mark wrote his gospel to open their eyes to Jesus' power and majesty. He shows Christ to be the Supreme Authority over all the earth, a powerful message to those living under one of the strongest empires the world has ever known.

Mark 1

More than any of the other gospels, Mark wants to plant you in the middle of the action as it takes place. That is why he uses terms like "immediately" and "suddenly" over and over. He also places a great deal of emphasis on Jesus' authority. The crowds who hear Jesus teach are amazed, for he teaches with real authority, unlike the teachers of the Law. Jesus also demonstrates his authority over demonic powers, diseases, sin, tradition, the Law, and the Sabbath. He possesses the power to forgive sin as well as command diseases to disappear. Mark wants us to understand that this is no ordinary man walking around Galilee. Jesus possesses an authority far greater than any earthly power, a point believers who live in the Roman emperor's shadow need to hear.

Mark 2–3

Jesus' healing the man on the Sabbath creates such a stir because of the rules the Jews had imposed on the day. The Old Testament simply says the day is to be a holy day of rest. Through the course of time, rabbis and religious teachers added to this. During the time between the Old and New Testaments, they came up with thirty-nine classes of actions that could not be done on the Sabbath. For example, they determined a person could not travel more than two thousand paces on the Sabbath. Any farther would constitute work and violate the day of rest. Listen closely to Jesus' words in 2:23–3:6. How should we treat this day of rest?

Mark 4

Verses 4:11-12 are very puzzling. Jesus taught in stories called parables. The stories all have a spiritual point. Chapter 4 contains four such stories. And that's why verses 11 and 12 are so puzzling. We think Jesus used stories because he was a great communicator (and he was). But these two verses tell us he used parables to keep people from understanding his message. He says, "They hear my words, but they don't understand. So they will not turn from their sins and be forgiven." Jesus quotes Isaiah 6:9-10 where God tells Isaiah to preach and "harden the hearts of these people. Close their ears, and shut their eyes." Would God really say that?

Whether we like it or not, he did. And Jesus repeated it. Why would God say something like this? To find the answer, you have to look at this from God's perspective. The good news of Jesus has two purposes, and it will always accomplish one or the other. When people hear it, some will understand and turn from their sins to Christ. For them the gospel is the power of God that saves them. Others will hear the same words and do nothing. After hearing the good news, they will walk away unchanged. The gospel leaves them without excuse as they stand before God. The gospel saves those who believe and condemns those who don't. Paul said much the same thing when he wrote:

> For the message of the cross is foolishness to those who are perishing, but to us who are being saved it is the power of God. For it is written:
>
> > "I will destroy the wisdom of the wise;
> > the intelligence of the intelligent I will frustrate."
> > (1 Corinthians 1:18-19, NIV)

By using parables, Jesus frustrated the "intelligence of the intelligent" while giving hope and life to those foolish enough to believe.

Mark 5

When God took on flesh and invaded the world through his Son, demonic forces lined up to oppose him. Some modern readers say that many of those the New Testament calls demon-possessed actually had psychological ailments. Mark 5 shows this was not the case. Notice how the demon-possessed man runs out to meet Jesus. Demonic forces recognize Jesus for who he truly is. Isn't it ironic that the Devil catches on before the religious leaders of the day? The demons identify themselves as "Legion." A legion was the largest unit of the Roman army, consisting of between three thousand and six thousand troops. Try to put yourself in the story as one of the pig herders. How would you react to seeing a herd of demon-possessed pigs charge over a cliff like lemmings?

Mark 6–7

The key word in the first half of Mark is authority. He shows how Jesus is greater than any king or empire or any other authority, visible or invisible, in all creation. Yet when Jesus goes back to his hometown, he is quickly dismissed as the carpenter's son. The people there have trouble believing the older brother of James, Joseph, Judas, and Simon could be anything more than a nail pounder. Familiarity breeds contempt, and not even Jesus' miracles can overcome their preconceived ideas about him. Not even his own family is convinced at first. Only after he rises from the dead do we see them become part of his disciples.

Verse 7:19 is the reason why you and I can eat pork and catfish and other animals the Law of Moses declared unclean. "By saying this, he [Jesus] showed that every kind of food is acceptable," the verse says. Before this point, the Jews would not eat anything that didn't have a cloven hoof or didn't chew its cud. Jesus moves beyond the "letter of the law" to God's intent. The Law never meant to imply that a person could be holy before God just by watching his or her diet. The real issue is not what goes into our bodies, but what comes out in our words and actions.

Mark 8

Mark 8:27-30 is the climax of the first half of Mark and the turning point of the book. Through his miracles and teaching, Jesus has shown his disciples who he is. Now for the test. Did they get it? From this point forward, Mark moves toward the cross. Jesus first predicts his death only after the disciples catch on that he is the Son of God. Now it will dominate his teaching.

Mark 9

Mark 9 gives us the greatest picture of the divine irony of Christ's life. In chapter 9, Jesus pulls back his humanity and allows three of his disciples to see his glory as God. Peter, James, and John can't even put into words the awe they felt in that moment. Not only do they see Jesus, they also see Moses and Elijah talking with him. With their appearance, Jesus shows how he is the fulfillment of all the Law and the Prophets. Immediately after this incredible appearance, Jesus takes the three back down the mountain to find a demon-possessed child waiting for him. Once again Jesus demonstrates his authority over the spiritual realm by driving the demon out with a spoken word.

Mark 10

In Mark 10, Jesus does more than perform miracles and teach the crowds. He tells us what is required to be his disciple. In his interaction with a group of children, his conversation with the rich young man, and his rebuke of the two disciples who wanted to sit at his right and left hand in his kingdom, Jesus tells us what is required of us if we truly want to follow him. Notice also how his description of his upcoming death becomes more and more graphic.

Mark 11–12

To grasp the full impact of the story of the evil farmers (Mark 12:1-11), read an earlier story about a vineyard found in Isaiah 5:1-7. Isaiah sang a song that compared the people of Israel and Judah to a vineyard. God himself planted the vineyard and expected it to produce sweet grapes. Instead, the grapes were wild and sour, completely useless for anything. The singer poses the question: What should God now do about this vineyard? All the farmers in the audience knew the answer. There was only one thing to do. The vineyard had to be totally destroyed and replanted with a fresh batch of vines.

The religious leaders to whom Jesus speaks know this song from Isaiah quite well. Throughout the Old Testament the Jews are compared to vineyards. Yet when Jesus tells the story of the evil farmers, he offers a twist from Isaiah's version. This time the vineyard isn't at fault; those who tended it are. Immediately the religious leaders know Jesus is talking about them. God has entrusted them with the spiritual care and nurture of the people. And they have failed. Rather than change when the Old Testament prophets rebuked them, they killed the messengers. No wonder this story so enrages them. They hear this poor carpenter blame them for all of the Jews' past spiritual failures. Not only that, he tells them they are no different than the evil kings and false prophets who led Israel and Judah into destruction in the Old Testament. That's why they hate Jesus. That's why they want him dead.

Mark 13

Mark 13 parallels Matthew 24, Luke 21, and Revelation 6. Jesus describes the events that will lead up to the time "when all of this will be fulfilled." "This" is the temple's destruction. Jesus predicts the magnificent buildings of the temple complex will be so completely demolished that not one stone would be left on top of another. Standing on the temple steps and gazing at the huge complex that had been under construction for nearly thirty years, the disciples can't fathom such a turn of events. "When will this happen?" they want to know. When Jesus answers them, he not only describes the signs preceding the destruction of the temple, but also the signs of his return and the end of the world.

Because Jesus answers a twofold question, his prophecies have double meaning and double fulfillments. The temple will be demolished just fewer than forty years after his conversation with his disciples. The Romans will destroy both the temple and most of the major Jewish cities. For those living in Jerusalem, it will be like the end of the world. Israel will cease to be a nation, and thousands of Jews will be killed. Not until 1948 will a Jewish state reappear in Palestine.

Yet, as you read Mark 13, you'll find that most of Jesus' words deal with his Second Coming. Verses 5-11 describe conditions that have existed since he first uttered these words. Rather than giving us clues for what to look for immediately prior to the Second Coming, Jesus tells us what we can expect while we wait for him. We will see wars and natural disasters, famine and persecution. As followers of Christ, we will be arrested, falsely accused, beaten, and killed. Even our own families will hate us because of Jesus. Yet he tells us not to fret. Instead, all of these will work together to provide a way for us to share our testimonies and glorify God. The history of Christianity has shown the gospel spreads fastest and churches are the strongest in times of trial, just as Jesus promises.

Mark 14–15

These chapters need to be read very slowly. The cross is central to the Christian life. Not only do Christ's death and resurrection bring us salvation and a new life with God, but Christ *is* our life. Listen to Paul: "And when Christ, who is your real life, is revealed to the whole world, you will share in all his glory" (Colossians 3:4). Slow down as you read Mark's account of the cross. Stop on each detail. Think about the physical pain Jesus felt. Let the agony of the cross sink in. Then prayerfully consider why Jesus went through such pain.

> Let us fix our eyes on Jesus, the author and perfecter of our faith, who for the joy set before him endured the cross, scorning its shame, and sat down at the right hand of the throne of God. Consider him who endured such opposition from sinful men, so that you will not grow weary and lose heart. (Hebrews 12:2-3, NIV)

Mark 16

When you reach chapter 16, you'll find a lot of footnotes that raise questions regarding the book's ending. Most translations of the Bible give two or three different endings for the book, along with some variation of the following footnote: "The most reliable early manuscripts conclude the gospel of Mark at verse 8.

Other manuscripts include various endings to the gospel." Does this mean we don't know how the book is supposed to end? The honest answer: yes. Before the invention of the printing press in the sixteenth century, books had to be copied by hand. Sometimes those doing the copying skipped a line or inserted something in the wrong place. By comparing manuscripts of various ages, biblical scholars are able to tell which is the closest to the original. This is called textual criticism.

God in his providence made sure there were plenty of copies to compare. Some go back to the early portions of the second century. Archaeologists have helped the process over the past two hundred years by discovering new caches of ancient documents. With all the handwritten copies found scattered across the three continents, very, very few variants have been found. The ending of Mark is the primary place where a large discrepancy exists. Why God allowed this to happen no one knows. Even with the variants, nothing in the other possible endings of Mark contradicts truths taught elsewhere in the New Testament. However, the discrepancies should make us even more cautious about basing our entire theology on these verses.

Luke

Unlike the writers of the other twenty-five books of the New Testament, Luke was not a Jew. He was a Gentile. While that term doesn't strike us as the stuff of prejudice, it did in the first century among those who worshiped the Lord God. In those days, the Jews divided the entire human race into one of two categories: Jews and Gentiles. According to the Jewish leaders of the first century, salvation belonged to the Jews alone. Everyone else was out of luck.

And that included Luke.

We do not know how Luke, who was most likely born to Greek parents, perhaps raised in the Syrian city of Antioch, came to Christ. The Bible never says. But this man the Jewish leaders would have kept at arm's length based solely upon his race became one of the key characters of the New Testament. Paul calls him a "dear friend" (Colossians 4:14, NIV). He proved himself to be a trusted coworker who accompanied Paul on many of his missionary journeys. In fact, when everyone else turned their backs on Paul shortly before the Roman government put him to death, Luke stayed at his side (2 Timothy 4:11). Paul also tells us Luke was a doctor, which explains the attention to detail we find in the two books he penned.

Luke's gospel and its companion volume, the book of Acts, make up one-fourth of the New Testament. Together they remind us that God's grace encompasses the entire earth. The plan God launched with Abraham and Sarah in the book of Genesis has always included both Jews and Gentiles. Now, in Christ, that barrier has been permanently removed. The world now consists of two categories of people: those who have been adopted into God's family through Christ, and those God would accept if they would only say yes to his Son.

LUKE AND THE OTHER GOSPELS

The book of Luke is very similar to Matthew and Mark. In places, the three are nearly identical. Scholars call them the Synoptic Gospels. *Synoptic* is Greek for "one view," and it means these three gospels tell the story of Christ's life from a similar point of view and with a similar structure. By contrast, John's gospel includes many stories the other three gospels don't include and follows a different structure.

Luke wrote both this gospel and the book of Acts. The first volume tells the life of Christ. The second picks up the story and tells of all God did through the followers of Jesus by the power of the Holy Spirit. Both were written from Rome while Paul sat in jail. Luke may well have written to show the Roman authorities the true nature of the Christian faith and to assure them that Christianity posed no political threat. Jesus didn't set out to build an earthly empire, and neither did his followers. The kingdom of God could never be confined to something so temporary, so eternally insignificant.

Luke 1–2

If this is your first trip through the New Testament, the first chapter of Luke may be a brand-new story you've never heard before. However, if you've ever watched *A Charlie Brown Christmas*, you've heard a major portion of the second chapter. It tells the Christmas story, beginning with the angel's visit to a young virgin named Mary. Only in Luke do we learn that Jesus was born in a barn and laid in a manger. We also hear the song of the angels in heaven as they announce the birth of the Savior of the world. Luke also includes a few details we don't usually hear about in the run-of-the-mill Christmas special. Two senior citizens see Jesus as an infant when his parents bring him to the temple for the first time, a devout man named Simeon and an old prophetess named Anna. As they behold the child, they both speak of what God will soon do through him. Both have waited for the Lord's Messiah their entire lives. After seeing Jesus, they can both die in peace, knowing God has at last heard their prayers.

Luke 3–4

The genealogy of Jesus in Luke differs from the one in Matthew. One traces his lineage through Mary, the other through Joseph. Many scholars believe Luke gives the former.[1]

Luke 4 records Jesus' first sermon. When he walks into a synagogue one Sabbath morning, he picks up one of the scrolls of Isaiah and reads the first few verses of chapter 61. Take a moment to turn back to Isaiah and read his prophecy there. After reading the text, Jesus gives a very simple message: "This Scripture has come true today before your very eyes!" At first the people think this is wonderful news, but Jesus doesn't stop there. Like John the Baptist before him, he confronts the people with their sin, specifically their sin of unbelief. By the time he is finished, the crowd wants to throw him off a cliff before his ministry even has time to start.

Luke 5–6

Listen closely to the Pharisees' response to Jesus and their growing tide of anger with him. Why do you think Jesus makes them so mad? How can they become upset when Jesus performs an amazing miracle, even if it does happen to be the Sabbath day when he does it? Do they honestly think Jesus should tell the man with the withered hand (6:6-11) to come back at a more convenient time? What can explain their reaction to the obvious display of the power of God in their midst?

Luke 7–8

Jesus finds himself at odds with the Pharisees and the crowds because of the things he says and the timing of his miracles. In these chapters, he also gets in trouble for the people he lets get close to him. Luke alone tells the story found in 7:36-50. It is very much like an incident that occurs shortly before Jesus goes to the cross (Matthew 26:6-13), but the two are not the same. Jesus defends the woman's action by giving us a simple, yet profound, principle: Those who have been forgiven for many sins often have greater love for God than those who have been forgiven only for little. This doesn't mean some of us are less bad than others in God's eyes. According to the book of Romans, all of us have sinned and deserve death and hell. The much and little in Luke 7 refer to the sinner's viewpoint. Those who think they are good enough on their own act like they're doing God a favor by serving him. Those who realize the depth of their depravity and the seriousness of their sin can hardly believe God would actually give them a second chance. As a result, they overflow with gratitude. It is the difference between the reaction of an outcast upon hearing he can now come into God's presence and those who think that position is theirs by right.

Luke 9

Luke 9:51 marks a turning point in the gospel's story. Jesus "resolutely set[s] out for Jerusalem." This isn't a sightseeing expedition. Nor does he plan to go to Jerusalem to socialize with old friends. From this point forward, Luke's gospel marches toward the cross. Everything you read from here on needs to be understood in this context. As Jesus travels from Galilee through Samaria to Judea and Jerusalem, he knows this will be the last time he will make this trip. Everything he does has a dual purpose of both fulfilling the reason behind his coming to earth and preparing his disciples for the work he would leave for them to fulfill.

Luke 10–11

The term "Good Samaritan" has been thrown around so much that it's easy to miss the story's impact. The Samaritans and Jews hated one another. The roots of their conflict go back hundreds of years, to 720 BC when the Assyrians invaded the northern kingdom of Israel. The Samaritans of Jesus' day were the descendants of the people the Assyrians moved to northern Palestine after they enslaved and carted off the Israelites to Assyria. The few remaining Israelites intermarried with the newcomers to form a new ethnic group that was neither truly Gentile nor completely Jewish. The Jews from the south despised them as half-breeds. When the Jews in the southern kingdom of Judah returned from their own seventy years of exile (600–530 BC), they rejected the Samaritans' offers of help. A little more than a hundred years later, the rift became complete, and the Samaritans built their own temple, complete with their own version of the Law. The hatred the Jews and Samaritans felt for one another is what makes the parable of the Good Samaritan so amazing.

Luke 12–13

As Jesus draws closer to Jerusalem, his message becomes clearer and clearer. Like John the Baptist before him, he doesn't soften the blow when it comes to what God requires. Anyone who wants to be his disciple must take up his cross and follow him. He didn't come to make the world happy or to bring about a giant party of peace and unity across the planet. Jesus divides people. He always has. He always will. That doesn't bother him. How could it? Jesus divides because most people will choose to stay in their sin rather than follow him. In Jesus' day, many of the worst sinners were outwardly the most religious.

Luke 14–16

Chapters 14–16 contain a collection of parables, most of which are found only in Luke. Several themes run through them, but one more than any other. Jesus tells these stories to show the distance between the self-righteous religious types and the despicable sinners and outcasts who welcome Jesus with open arms. The Pharisees view the tax collectors and sinners as scum to be avoided. Jesus sees them as lost sheep, a lost coin, and a lost son. He sees value in those the world throws away. This as much as anything contributes to the anger that keeps growing among the Pharisees. Their entire system is built on performance. Jesus comes bringing grace. Sadly, the Pharisees never realize how much they have in common with those they reject.

The parable of the shrewd manager in chapter 16 strikes most readers as off-kilter. Why would Jesus praise a man who was obviously dishonest? What does Jesus want us to learn from the man's actions? The answer is there in the text. Do you see it? Look at the entire context. What is Jesus saying through this parable?

Luke 17–18

Faith plays a key role in Jesus' teaching in chapter 18. He shares two parables about prayer, which are followed by two stories of people coming to Jesus. As you read, pay close attention to the lessons of each. Based on the story of the persistent widow and the story of the Pharisee and the tax collector, what do we need to do for our prayers to be heard? Then, based on the stories of the children coming to Jesus and the rich young man, what does it take for us to be accepted by Jesus? What is the key difference between the children and the rich man? Before you pass over the rich man's story too quickly, ask yourself whether Jesus' demand seems reasonable. If you were in the man's place, what would you think when you heard Jesus say, "Sell all you have and give the money to the poor"? Why would Jesus ask this guy to do such a thing? How does that apply to us today? Does this mean we need to get rid of all our stuff and give it to the poor before we can be saved? Why or why not?

Luke 19

Luke 19:41-44 refers to events that will take place in Jerusalem forty years after Jesus' execution. The Jews will revolt against Rome, and Rome will annihilate their nation and turn Jerusalem to rubble.

Some commentators think these verses prove that Luke is writing this gospel some time after the destruction of Jerusalem in 70 AD. However, because Luke is writing his gospel shortly before writing Acts, and Paul is still alive at the end of the book of Acts, this is unlikely. Paul will die around 64 or 65 AD as a result of Nero's persecution. Luke isn't putting words into Jesus' mouth to make him talk about something Luke has experienced. Instead, Jesus as the Son of God and Prophet of God knows what will soon take place. And that thought fills him with grief. Even though he knows the Jews will reject him and put him to death, he loves them. That's why he will die for them.

Luke 20–21

The story of the widow's small offering appears only in Mark and Luke. The story by itself stands as one of the greatest commentaries ever on the subject of giving. However, taken together with the string of stories focused on money that Luke has included over the past several chapters, its significance becomes even clearer. Luke 16:14 describes the Pharisees as a money-obsessed bunch. They love their cash, even going so far as to twist around the rules of giving to God to put more of it in their own pockets. The action of the widow who put her two small copper coins into the collection box puts all of the religious experts to shame. She did voluntarily the very thing Jesus demanded of the rich young man.

Luke 22

Does Jesus advocate the use of violence in verses 35-38? And if not, why does he tell his disciples to make sure they have a sword with them? Part of the answer lies in the number of swords the disciples have among them. When Jesus tells them to sell their clothes to buy a sword if they need to, they reply, "Lord, we have two swords among us." Jesus says, "That is enough." Two swords are enough for Jesus to make his point, but they certainly are not enough for twelve men to defend themselves against an armed mob. By telling the disciples to bring along the two swords, Jesus in effect warns them that they now face a life-and-death situation. Then, when he refuses to allow the disciples to fight back, he reassures his followers that he has chosen this path voluntarily.

Luke 23

Luke includes details regarding Jesus' trial that we don't find anywhere else. We know from the other gospel accounts that

Jesus stood before Pilate and that Pilate didn't want to have to make a decision on this matter. Only in Luke do we discover how far Pilate would go to try to rid himself of responsibility in this case. As soon as he hears Jesus is from Galilee, Pilate sends him off to stand trial before Herod. Luke 23:8 says Herod was "delighted at the opportunity to see Jesus." Word of his miracles had spread throughout every circle in the region. Herod doesn't want to learn more about obtaining eternal life. He just wants to see Jesus perform a miracle or two. When Jesus won't play along, Herod dresses him in a royal robe to mock him, then sends him back to Pilate for execution.

The story of the conversion of the thief on the cross appears only in Luke 23:39-43.

Luke 24

Why does Jesus eat a piece of fish in verses 42-43? The answer lies in verse 37. The disciples still can't believe their eyes. They think they are seeing a ghost. But Jesus isn't a ghost. His body is real, not a phantom. By eating solid food he demonstrates this fact to his followers. However, his body differs in its resurrection state from its pre-cross form. He no longer needs doors to enter a room. The physical world no longer holds him in its grip. Far from being a ghost, he is now more real than he has ever been before, because his body can no longer be affected by things like sickness and death. To learn more about how Jesus' resurrection body is a promise to us, see 1 John 3:2.

John

When God appeared to Moses at the burning bush and told him to go to Pharaoh and demand freedom for the Hebrew slaves, Moses asked God, "Suppose I go to the Israelites and say to them, 'The God of your fathers has sent me to you,' and they ask me, 'What is his name?' Then what shall I tell them?" (Exodus 3:13, NIV)

"I AM WHO I AM," the Lord replied. "This is what you are to say to the Israelites: 'I AM has sent me to you'" (verse 14, NIV).

John set out to answer the same question Moses asked, but in a slightly different form. Moses wanted to know the name of the one true God, the God of his fathers. John writes so his readers will discover the true identity of Jesus of Nazareth. God said his name would be the same from generation to generation. To Moses he revealed himself by the name I AM. Fourteen hundred years later, Jesus revealed himself to both his disciples and his opponents by the same name. His critics asked Jesus how he could dare compare himself to Abraham. He simply replied, "Before Abraham was born, I am!" (John 8:58, NIV). The God of the burning bush was now on earth in human flesh.

This is the message of the fourth gospel.

Perhaps as many as thirty years passed between the time Mark wrote the first gospel and John wrote the last. By the time the Spirit moved John to write, the other three gospels had a fairly wide circulation among the churches. This left John free to expand on what the others wrote and to fill in some of the gaps in the story. At times it feels as though John starts right where the others stop. For example, Luke tells how the disciples argued among themselves over who was greatest as they sat down with Jesus to eat the final Passover meal. John doesn't include this detail. Instead, he picks up where Luke stops and tells how Jesus answered their arguments by washing the disciples' feet.

John also focuses on the private conversations Jesus had with both his followers and his enemies, rather than the sermons he delivered to the crowds. That's why we don't hear the Sermon on the Mount in John, but we do hear his conversations with Nicodemus in the middle of the night and the Samaritan woman next to a well. By themselves, none of the four Gospels is complete. Only by reading them all do we get the full picture of what Jesus did when he walked on earth. Even then our knowledge is incomplete. John put it this way, "I suppose that if all the other things Jesus did were written down, the whole world could not contain the books" (John 21:25).

John 1–2

John includes only eight miracles, one of which occurs after Jesus rose from the dead. Each one acts as a sign, pointing people to Jesus' true nature. The first of the eight appears in chapter 2. Also in chapter 2 you find Jesus clearing the moneychangers out of the temple. The other gospels put this at the end of Jesus' life, when he enters Jerusalem on a donkey as the crowds cry, "Hosanna!" Why the discrepancy? The best answer is the obvious one. Jesus' ministry on earth lasted three years. As a Jew, he went to Jerusalem for the Passover each year. The episode in John 2 took place a year or two before the one recorded in the other gospels. If Jesus found people turning his Father's house into a marketplace, he would do something about it. And when they returned, he did something about it a second time.

John 3–4

The central characters in these two chapters couldn't be more different. Nicodemus is a religious leader of the Jewish people. He knows the Old Testament and the Law inside and out. Yet he still feels compelled to come to Jesus. The woman at the well in John 4 is an outcast among outcasts. By all rights, Jesus shouldn't even talk to her. After all, she is a Samaritan and he is a Jew. To say the two races hate each other is an understatement. On top of that, she has a reputation. Divorced five times, she now lives with a man to whom she isn't married. Attitudes toward that kind of behavior in the first century were a little different than today. Unlike Nicodemus, she doesn't go looking for Jesus. He comes looking for her. As you read, listen to what each story has to say about God's plan of salvation and his grace.

John 5–6

When Jesus calls God his Father in 5:18, he makes himself equal with God. The Pharisees hear this claim and want to kill him as a heretic. He then goes on to show how the Scriptures (and by this, Jesus means the Old Testament) point to him as the Messiah. Put yourself in the Pharisees' position. How would his words sound to you?

Jesus never plays to the crowd. He knows how people are. In 5:41 he tells his critics their approval means nothing to him. Apparently he feels this way about all people. He doesn't need their approval, only his Father's. This point becomes very clear toward the end of chapter 6. Huge crowds follow Jesus in hopes of seeing a miracle. But they don't stick around. Pay close attention to his interaction with his disciples in 6:60-71. Also, chapter 6 contains one of Jesus' I AM statements. When he calls himself the Bread of Life, he is equating himself with the manna that came from heaven in the wilderness during the Exodus.

John 7–8

John 8:52-58 plays a major role in our understanding of Jesus as God, especially verse 58. A literal translation reads, "Truly, truly, before Abraham was, I AM." Jesus makes more than a statement about his relationship with Abraham. By choosing the words, "I AM," he clearly makes a claim about who he is. The Pharisees don't miss what he is saying. That's why they are ready to execute him right then and there. Jesus not only claims to be the I AM of Exodus 3, he is in effect claiming the most personal name of God as his own. Either he is completely out of his gourd, or he is who he claims to be.

John 9–10

John writes with an incredible sense of irony in the story of the man born blind. If you miss the humor, reread the story. Just in case you still don't see it (pun intended), listen to the Pharisees' conversation with the miracle man. More than just Jesus' miracle of opening the man's eyes allows God's glory to shine in this guy. His response to the miracle and his interaction with the Pharisees do as well.

Chapter 10 is a great passage for those who want proof of who Jesus is. People asked for the same evidence when he walked on earth. The proof lies in what he does in his Father's name, both as recorded in the Bible and in the lives of people today.

John 11–12

John 11:35 is the shortest verse in the Bible, and perhaps one of the hardest to understand. If Jesus plans on raising Lazarus from the dead, why does he weep? What moves him to tears? Perhaps the biggest question lies in the reaction of the chief priests and Pharisees. Why would they want to kill a man who could raise people from the dead? Think about the divine irony in this. If Jesus can raise people from the dead, how effective will death be as a weapon against him? They should know he himself will rise. Notice how Jesus waits until Lazarus is not only dead, but also buried away and starting to decay. If he can order the grave to release those upon whom it has this kind of grip, how can the grave possibly keep him?

John 12:37-40 sounds like a contradiction of all we know about God. Why would he keep people from understanding who Jesus was? John quotes Isaiah 53:1 and 6:10. Go back and read them in their original context. By quoting the prophets, John shows how the response of the Jews to Jesus fell in line with the way their forefathers reacted to God's prophets. Before you jump to the conclusion that God is unfair, reread John 3:19. Compare it to Jonah 2:8: "Those who cling to worthless idols forfeit the grace that could be theirs" (NIV). What do these verses say about God's willingness to forgive and mankind's willingness to turn from sin?

John 13–14

John 13 marks the beginning of Jesus' final day on earth. If you had only one day left to live, what would you do? How does this compare with what Jesus did in 13:1-5?

Beginning with 13:31 and continuing on to the end of chapter 17, John gives us Jesus' final words to his disciples. Last words and final actions say a lot about a person's character. What do these say about Jesus' character? As you read, note the number of promises Jesus makes in these chapters. Where is his focus as he moves toward the cross?

John 15–17

In chapters 15–16, Jesus promises to give us everything we need to live for him and to make a difference in this world. He also tells us what we can expect as we walk through this world. Of all the promises made in these two chapters, perhaps the greatest is found in 16:33, "I have told you all this so that you may have peace in me. Here on earth you will have many trials and sorrows. But take heart, because I have overcome the world." He strips away all the delusions of finding paradise on this earth. As long as we live here, we will have sorrows. But there's no need to worry. Jesus overcame this world. Notice the verbs all appear in the present tense even though Jesus had not yet risen from the dead, the act by which he conquered sin and death and Satan once and for all.

John 18–19

Throughout John's gospel, he gives details of private conversations Jesus had with both his followers and his opponents. In his account of Jesus' trial in chapters 18–19, John does this again by taking us inside Jesus' conversations with Pilate. As you read, you sense how Pilate's authority pales in comparison with that of Jesus. You also hear some of Pilate's frustration, not only with Jesus, but also with the circumstances swirling around him. His question in 18:38 rings louder today than when it was first uttered: "What is truth?" The world still struggles to find the answer even though he stands right in front of them.

John includes other details we don't find anywhere else, including Jesus entrusting John with the care of his mother,

Mary. We also learn that Joseph of Arimathea doesn't act alone when he takes Jesus' body down from the cross and lays it in his own tomb. One of the members of the Jewish council helps him, a man we met in John 3, Nicodemus.

John 20–21

John gives us a rare peek into Jesus' interaction with the disciples after his resurrection. For forty days, he meets with them and explains how the Law and the Prophets all pointed to the necessity of his death and resurrection. Pay particular attention to Jesus' conversation with Peter and to his statement about the "disciple . . . whom Jesus loved" — John. Think about this statement in light of the last book John wrote, the book of Revelation.

Acts

Luke wrote Acts shortly after completing the third gospel, probably around the year 64. His second volume tells the story of the first thirty years of the church's history, but it does far more than that. This is no cold tale of dates and places. Instead, Acts shows how Jesus continued to work on earth through the Holy Spirit he sent after he ascended into heaven. Jesus was just getting started during his three years of ministry in a human body. After he rose again, he breathed power into his followers and set them on fire with a flame from heaven. Throughout the centuries, the enemies of God have tried to douse the flame, but the more they fight against it, the brighter it burns and the farther it spreads. What has proved to be true over the past two thousand years can first be found in Acts, where the Jews, the Romans, and even Ephesian shopkeepers tried to silence Jesus' followers. They couldn't then, and no one can now.

The new work Christ does through his church eliminates old labels like Jew and Gentile, rich and poor, slave and free. As a result, the promise God made to Abraham in Genesis 12 finally comes true. The entire world will now be blessed through the descendants of Abraham who, like the patriarch, believe the good news and have it counted to them as righteousness.

Acts 1–2

What really happens to Judas? The Gospels say he goes out and hangs himself, while Acts says he buys a field with the money he received, where he falls over and bursts open, spilling out his intestines. Which account is correct? They both are. Once Judas realizes what he has done, he throws the thirty pieces of silver at the chief priests. The money cannot be returned to the temple treasury because it is blood money, so the priests buy a field in Judas's name. Why do they choose the field they do? Because that is the place where Judas committed suicide. He hangs himself there. After a time, the rope breaks, or the knot gives way, or something else happens that causes his dead, decaying body to fall to the ground. When it does, it bursts open from the swelling caused by the gases the process of decay produces. The story is not for the faint of heart.

Acts 2 marks a major turning point in the way God works in the world. Before this time, the Holy Spirit did not permanently reside in human beings. The Lord sent his Spirit upon people at certain times throughout Israel's history to equip them for a specific work he had in store for them (see Exodus 31:3 and Judges 3:10). However, through the prophets, God vowed to do something radically different. In Jeremiah 31:31-33, God promised a new covenant where he would write his laws upon the hearts of believers. And in Joel 2:28-29, he promised to pour out his Spirit on all people. Both of these promises come true on the day of Pentecost. God pours out his Spirit so that now all believers have the Spirit of God living inside of them.

Luke tells us that "everyone present was filled with the Holy Spirit and began speaking in other languages, as the Holy Spirit gave them this ability" (Acts 2:4). The people who come running hear these believers speaking in specific, known languages. When the Holy Spirit comes on the believers, they start prophesying—that is, they boldly proclaim God's message. Because the Feast of Pentecost is going on, Jerusalem is filled with pilgrims from across the Roman Empire. God makes sure these pilgrims hear the gospel in their native tongues by giving the disciples the ability to speak in languages they have never learned.

Acts 3–4

Acts 3 contains a simple summary of the good news about Jesus: He was God's Messiah, but instead of welcoming him, the Jews killed him. However, he wouldn't stay dead. God raised him up, fulfilling everything he promised to do through the prophets. Now people everywhere must turn from their sins and to Christ. That is, in a nutshell, the message of Jesus.

Acts 4 shows the tension between the power of the gospel and the hardness of human hearts. Instead of welcoming the good news, the Jewish leaders arrest the disciples, just as they had arrested Jesus. Pay close attention to the reactions of Peter, John, and the church as a whole. Notice how the church prays after their leaders are arrested. What do they not pray for? What would you pray for if you faced the same situation? Acts 4:32-37 describes the community the earliest disciples enjoy. It shows how we are to share one another's burdens.

Acts 5

Is God a little severe in his dealings with Ananias and Sapphira? Do they really need to die? How can you reconcile such extreme action with the God of love? To help find the answers, read Leviticus 9–10. The real action takes place in chapter 10, but you won't see the significance of it unless you read chapter 9 as well. God's response to Aaron's sons parallels Acts 5. Both chapters mark the beginning of a new work God is doing among people. In Leviticus 9 the tabernacle has just been dedicated, and the priests have interceded for the people for the first time. What happens on that day will set the tone for the rest of Israel's history as they approach God. The same goes with Acts 5. The Holy Spirit has just been poured out on all people. He now fills every believer just as he filled the tabernacle in the

Old Testament. That is why God's response to sin on these two days is so similar.

Acts 6–7

Stephen's speech in chapter 7 is the longest in the book of Acts. In it we see how everything God did in the Old Testament pointed toward what he would one day do in Christ. But we also see in Stephen how God's Spirit carries us and sustains us when we face opposition. Jesus told his disciples not to worry about what they would say when they were dragged in front of courts and councils, because the Holy Spirit would tell them what to say. This chapter is just one example of this promise coming true. Stephen most likely already knows the facts he shares in his defense speech, but God brings it all together, along with peace and grace, when most of us would freeze up. Notice how the Jewish leaders react to everything he says.

Acts 8–9

The first verse of chapter 8 should go with chapter 7. It is almost an aside, just a little extra detail thrown in, but it foreshadows what will take place in the rest of the story. As the crowd rushes at Stephen to stone him to death, they throw their coats at the feet of a young man named Saul. Apparently he is there for the entire trial. He hears every word Stephen says. Keep this in mind as you read chapter 9.

Acts 10–12

From the beginning of time, the Lord's plan included the entire world. When he revealed himself to Abraham and his descendants, God planned for them to be a light to the nations. After struggling with idolatry throughout their first fifteen hundred years, the Jews basically decided the only way to stay pure was to avoid contact with the Gentile world. The Pharisees, with their extra rules on what constituted "clean" and "unclean," solidified this conviction. Jesus didn't share this attitude. He healed the servant of a Roman officer and cast a demon out of the daughter of a woman from Tyre (in modern Lebanon). Although he made it clear he had come for the lost sheep of Israel, he also hinted that eventually the entire world would come to him. That time arrives in these chapters.

Even though the Jews separate themselves from the Gentiles, they do allow converts to join them after a rigorous conversion process. Gentiles who have not converted but who are attracted to the God of Israel are known as God-fearers. They worship the God of Israel but have not gone through the conversion rituals. We are introduced to one in chapter 10, a man named Cornelius. This chapter describes how and why the gospel spread to people like us, those born outside Judaism.

Acts 13–14

These chapters chronicle the first of Paul's missionary journeys. He goes along with Barnabas, the man who welcomed him when all the other disciples were afraid of him. Barnabas's cousin John Mark accompanies them. He can't take the rigors of the road, however, and goes back home. This event plays a major role in the next chapter.

Chapter 13 contains one of Paul's longest recorded sermons. Luke includes it here to give us a taste of what Paul said when he proclaimed Jesus in the synagogues. Like Peter and Stephen, Paul shows how Jesus fulfills the promises God made throughout the Old Testament. All of these men saw Christ's work as an extension of what God had done before, rather than a radical change of his eternal plans. As you read, pay close attention to the role of women and the place of suffering in the Christian life.

Acts 15

When God throws the doors of the church open to Gentiles, he leaves a question hanging over the church: Do Gentiles who come to Christ also need to convert to Judaism? If not, how much of the Law does one have to obey to be called a true believer? This question is the central issue of the council that meets in Acts 15. For more insight into this question, read the book of Galatians. Paul wrote it shortly before the events of this chapter.

Acts 16–18

These three chapters detail Paul's second missionary journey. Keep in mind that modern forms of travel had not yet been invented. Aside from the few times Paul and his companions travel by boat, they walk everywhere they go. These aren't two-week mission trips. Instead, Paul's team spends months slogging through difficult terrain filled with dangers, not to mention the opposition they encounter in the major cities.

Barnabas has gone off to lead a separate mission team, and now Paul's main partner is a man named Silas. Early in their trip they meet the teenaged Timothy, and he joins their party. Eventually Luke too signs on. We know this because the references to Paul's traveling party change from "they" to "we," indicating that the author of Acts has gone with them.

Acts 19–20

Ephesus was the center of worship of Artemis, also known as Diana. A fertility goddess, Artemis's statues showed her covered with breasts to nurse and care for all of nature. The largest and greatest temple to Artemis sat in Ephesus. One of the seven wonders of the ancient world, the temple was built of marble and was 342 feet long and 164 feet across, with columns 56 feet high surrounding it. In the center sat a shrine hidden by curtains. Within the center shrine the Ephesians guarded an ancient image of the goddess that was said to have fallen from heaven. Most likely a meteorite, this relic set Ephesus apart, making it the place to which worshipers made pilgrimages.

This bit of background information should help you understand the riot that breaks out in the second half of chapter 19. Artemis wasn't just spiritually important to Ephesus. Tourists flocking to her temple helped feed the local economy. Souvenir shops sold small silver reproductions of Artemis herself. When more and more people turned to Christ, demand for Artemis products dropped, and the economy suffered as a result. That is why the local merchants felt they had to do something to stop the spread of Christianity.

Acts 21–22

When Paul goes to the temple with the four men completing their vows, he pays for the sacrifices the Law requires. This raises a difficult question. How could Paul write that we are free from the Law (Romans 6:14) and later follow the Law by offering sacrifices for these men? Paul's actions would contradict his words if he were keeping this part of the Law in order to win favor with God or to be saved. Yet the text is clear that neither is the case. He pays for the expenses of the sacrifices for these men to keep peace within the church in Jerusalem and with Jewish believers. Jews who came to Christ did not stop thinking of themselves as Jews. Nor did they abandon the temple and the other parts of their heritage with which they grew up. Their faith rested not on their ability to observe the Law, but in Jesus Christ. In fact, they saw themselves as the truest of Jews, for they had embraced God's Messiah. Paul's actions are not some sort of compromise with the Jewish leaders who rejected Jesus. Rather, he accommodates his brothers and sisters in Christ in Jerusalem to keep peace within the family. Acts 21 is an example of Paul becoming all things to all men to win some (1 Corinthians 9:22).

Acts 23–24

These chapters may look like wasted time in Paul's life. After all, he spends two years in jail in Caesarea without any real charges filed against him. The only charges come from the Jewish religious leaders, yet these charges don't have any bearing in the Roman legal system. The governor, Felix, keeps Paul in prison partly as a favor to the Jewish leaders, and partly because he thinks Paul will pay a bribe to win his release. Hoping for a bribe, Felix sends for Paul often. Rather than pay up, Paul shares Christ with him.

Before Paul's life becomes bogged down in this process, Jesus appears to him and reassures him of his ultimate plan. How will this vision encourage Paul in the coming months? What does this say about the unexpected detours and delays our lives hit? What does this also say about what it means to be in the middle of God's will?

Acts 25–26

Paul finally has to appeal to have his case heard by Caesar himself. That is his right as a Roman citizen. Appealing to Caesar is the only way Paul can keep from being sent back to the Jewish leaders in Jerusalem. Ironically, the next Roman authority to hear his case, Agrippa, would have set Paul free if Paul hadn't appealed to Caesar. So the thing that keeps him from being killed by the Jews now prevents him from winning his freedom. For Paul, all this means he will be sent to Rome at Rome's expense. God has a funny way of getting his will done.

Acts 27–28

Acts ends without resolving Paul's case. Most likely this is because he was still awaiting his hearing before Caesar when Luke wrote the book. Some have speculated that Luke wrote Acts in part to help Paul's case. The book shows that Christianity poses no political threats to the Romans. For us, the book shows how God controls every situation. No matter how high the obstacles, no matter how great the opposition may be, God will prevail. Chapter 27 is a fitting reminder of this fact.

Letters from Home

Romans, First and Second Corinthians,
Galatians, Ephesians, Philippians,
Colossians, First and Second Thessalonians,
First and Second Timothy, Titus, Philemon,
Hebrews, James, First and Second Peter,
First, Second, and Third John, Jude, Revelation

AUTHORS

Paul wrote the first thirteen letters. James, Peter, John, and Jude wrote the letters that bear their name. John also penned Revelation. Hebrews doesn't name an author, nor can scholars definitively say who wrote it.

WHEN WERE THESE BOOKS WRITTEN?

They cover a fifty-year period between AD 45, when James wrote the first letter, and AD 95, when John wrote Revelation.

WHAT ARE THEY ABOUT?

As the title above states, this is a collection of letters. At least twenty-four of the twenty-seven books of the New Testament are written as direct correspondence from one person to another. The first thirteen in this section, all written by Paul, bear the names of their recipients, as does the anonymous book of Hebrews. The next seven bear the name of the author, while Revelation stands apart as a unique case.

Because the New Testament is a collection of letters for all believers at all times, each one of us can put our own name in the address line. Paul might have written the book of Romans to Christians living in the capital city of the ancient empire, yet God also had you and me in mind. This collection of twenty-seven books is a set of letters from home, sent from God's heart to yours. Yet he didn't write them to you alone. He sent these letters to every person who believes in Jesus Christ as his or her Savior. As if to emphasize this point, the plural use of the word "you" in Romans through Jude outnumbers the singular use 916 to 250. When the books written to individuals are excluded, the ratio grows to 898 to 110. God isn't just addressing individuals walking alone with him. He speaks to all of us as a community.

Therefore, as you read each book of the New Testament, you read with a crowd that stretches out over time and space. God speaks to you through the book of Romans just as he spoke to the people who read the letter for the first time. And he speaks to you just as he speaks to a brother or sister in Christ reading the same verses in China or India or Nigeria or across the street from your house. Sitting in the middle of this crowd listening to God forces us to ask ourselves more than, *What does God want* me *to do with what I am reading today?* Together we need to ask, *What does he want* us *to do? How can we live out these truths together?*

Romans

From: Paul

To: Believers in the city of Rome, both Jews and Gentiles, whom Paul had never met face-to-face.

Why did he write? To explain fully the good news of Jesus he preached.

First and Second Corinthians

From: Paul

To: The church in Corinth, which Paul started on his second missionary journey.

Why did he write? To correct the rash of problems that had broken out in the church.

Galatians

From: Paul

To: Believers throughout Galatia (in the middle of modern Turkey), where Paul traveled on his first and second missionary journeys.

Why did he write? To explain the relationship between grace and the law.

Ephesians

From: Paul

To: The church in the city of Ephesus, where Paul spent two years during his third missionary journey.

Why did he write? To explain the mystery of how God's eternal plan came together in Christ and how believers fit into this plan.

Philippians

From: Paul

To: The church in the city of Philippi, the first city in Europe to hear Paul's message during his second missionary journey.

Why did he write? To thank the Philippians for their financial gift and to encourage them to rejoice in Christ regardless of what they may be going through.

Colossians

From: Paul

To: The church in the city of Colossae.

Why did he write? To combat a growing heresy that denied the full deity and humanity of Jesus.

First and Second Thessalonians

From: Paul

To: The church in the city of Thessalonica.

Why did he write? To encourage those who were suffering for their faith.

First and Second Timothy

From: Paul

To: Timothy, the pastor of the church in Ephesus and one of Paul's apprentices.

Why did he write? To encourage and instruct Timothy as he led the church in Ephesus.

Titus

From: Paul

To: Titus, a young pastor Paul trained and sent to serve on the island of Crete.

Why did he write? To tell Titus how to give order to the church on Crete.

Philemon

From: Paul

To: Philemon, a believer in the church in Colossae whom Paul led to Christ.

Why did he write? To encourage Philemon to forgive and welcome back his runaway slave and fellow believer, Onesimus.

Hebrews

From: An unnamed church leader who was in Rome when he wrote the letter.

To: Jewish believers.

Why did he write? To encourage believers to stick with Jesus rather than turning back to the Jewish system in the face of persecution.

James

From: James, the brother of Jesus and pastor of the church in Jerusalem.

To: Jewish believers scattered across the nations.

Why did he write? To show how real faith demands a changed life.

First and Second Peter

From: Peter

To: Believers scattered across Asia Minor (modern Turkey), both Jews and Gentiles.

Why did he write? To encourage those suffering for their faith and to warn them about false teachers infiltrating the ranks of believers.

First, Second, and Third John
From: John

To: Believers in an unnamed location, perhaps Ephesus. Third John is addressed to a man named Gaius.

Why did he write? To reaffirm the truth that Jesus is fully human and fully God, a truth that false teachers regularly attacked.

Jude
From: Jude, another brother of Jesus.

To: Believers in an unnamed location.

Why did he write? To warn against false teachers and to encourage true believers to remain faithful to Jesus.

Revelation
From: John

To: Believers in the cities of Ephesus, Smyrna, Pergamum, Thyatira, Sardis, Philadelphia, and Laodicea, all of which were in Asia Minor (Turkey).

Why did he write? To deliver the revelation of the events surrounding the second coming of Jesus and encourage believers suffering persecution.

Romans

The book of Romans reads less like a letter and more like a full explanation of all Paul believes. He wrote the letter to the followers of Jesus who lived in Rome, even though he had never personally met them. Unlike Galatians, Thessalonians, or Corinthians, Paul didn't start the church to which he wrote. No one knows who first planted Christianity in the capital of the empire. It probably landed there after a group of unnamed Jews who first heard the gospel on the day of Pentecost went back home after their pilgrimage (Acts 2). Paul wrote this letter to introduce himself to the believers there. No doubt they had heard a lot about the man who traveled from city to city telling others about Jesus. Regrettably, not all of the information they received was accurate. Paul wrote to them while visiting Corinth shortly after writing 2 Corinthians (sometime early in AD 57). He wanted to let them know how much he wanted to visit them. But more than that, he wanted to make it clear that he faithfully taught the truth of Jesus Christ.

Romans 1–2

Before we can understand the good news of salvation through Christ, we must first come to grips with the bad news of the human condition. After a brief introduction in 1:1-17, Paul shoves a mirror in the reader's face. Romans 1:18-32 shows the entire human race as sinners in desperate need of a Savior. Paul describes how God has revealed himself to all the earth through nature, yet the human race chose to worship creation rather than the Creator. These verses also reveal the way God judges sin. Instead of striking us with lightning bolts, he allows us to fall deeper and deeper into the pit we as a species dig for ourselves. If we ever wonder why our world is in the shape it is in, we simply need to read Romans 1.

Chapter 2 shows how religious people are no better off. The Jews think they are just fine in their relationship with God because they have the Law and observe the ordinance of circumcision. Paul strips them of their confidence and shows how nothing done in the flesh can overcome the problem of sin. It isn't just that performance can't earn God's salvation. A far greater problem confronts us. None of us, no matter how strong our will or firm our resolve, can keep the Law. Instead, we end up doing the very things we condemn in others even though we know better. In some ways chapter 2 sums up the conclusion of the Old Testament.

Romans 3–4

The picture of the human race drawn in 1:18–3:18 is so grim, so hopeless, we're left wondering if anything can deliver us from the pit of sin the human race dug for itself. Only one hope can be found, only one way whereby we can be forgiven and restored to a right relationship with God: Jesus Christ. Verse 3:19 shows the role the Law plays in all of this. We sometimes get so used to being forgiven that we pass right over the wonder of 3:23-28. Read it slowly and let it soak in. These verses tell us why Jesus had to die and how wonderful God's grace truly is.

Chapter 4 shows how God's plan has been the same since the beginning of time. The good news of Jesus wasn't some sort of "plan B" God threw together when the Law of Moses didn't work. Just the opposite is the case. The Law worked perfectly by showing us our utter sinfulness. It reveals how no one will ever earn God's approval by performance. Instead of making promises and crawling fifty miles on our knees to show

how sincere we are, we must do what Abraham did. We must believe. Chapter 4 shows how the gospel is a continuation and fulfillment of what came before in the Old Testament.

Romans 5–6

Romans 5:12-21 explains why the story of Genesis 1–3 must be true. If Adam was not a real historical figure, then this chapter falls apart as meaningless. If creation is nothing more than the end result of random events, and if the human race gradually evolved from lower life forms, sin doesn't exist and Jesus didn't need to come to earth. Since Paul shows how Jesus is the second Adam, the first Adam must be a historical figure, not a myth. Adam's act of disobedience brought death to the entire human race. Jesus' act of obedience gives life to everyone who will believe. For the second to be true, the first must be true.

Chapter 6 addresses a common question among believers. If grace is so strong and God's forgiveness so complete, does this mean we should just keep on sinning so we can experience even more of God's grace? Chapter 6 gives Paul's answer. Freedom in Christ doesn't mean freedom to keep on disgracing God's name. Instead, it is a freedom to serve him fully and completely without fear. When a person has been born again, he will long to please Christ (2 Corinthians 5:17). We are set free from our slavery to sin so we can live for God.

Romans 7–8

Chapter 7 reveals the purpose of the Law. God never intended for it to be a means by which people could earn his favor. Instead, he gave it to us as a gift, to help us understand the depths of our sinfulness. Without it, we would walk around under the delusion that we're pretty good people.

Chapter 8 explains how the Holy Spirit can do in us what the Law can't: He can change us from the inside out so we think God's thoughts and do his will. Change happens by God's grace, but it requires our active cooperation.

Some of the Bible's greatest promises are in chapter 8. We find both the wonder of life in the Spirit and the depths of God's love for us. As you read 8:31-39, think about the ways God already showed this promise to be true through the story of Israel in the Old Testament. If nothing could separate them from God's love in spite of their best efforts to wiggle out of his grip, how much greater is this promise to those of us who have found new life in Christ?

Romans 9–11

Chapter 9 is built firmly on the Law and the Prophets of the Old Testament. In this chapter we come face-to-face with God's power and sovereignty. We think of him as the God of the second chance, but these verses remind us that we don't deserve anything from God except condemnation. He showers his favor on those who believe because he chooses to, not because he must. Don't pass too quickly over the questions Paul raises in this chapter. Stop and ponder them. What do these verses tell us about God, people, and the question of fairness? Do we really want God to play fair?

To fully understand chapter 11, you need to think in terms of the Old Testament plotline and God's purpose in selecting Abraham and his descendants. This chapter demonstrates how the New Testament is a continuation of the story God started writing in the book of Genesis and continued throughout the Law, the Prophets, and the Writings. God didn't do something radically new and different in Jesus.

Instead, through his Son he finished what he started in the very beginning of time.

Romans 12–16

These chapters explore the practical implications of life in Christ. The only sane response to grace is to live like this. Romans 8 tells how the Holy Spirit works in the life of a believer who actively cooperates with him. Chapters 12–15 outline some of the habits that cooperating with the Holy Spirit will produce. They include ways of relating to fellow believers and to those outside the faith.

Pay close attention to the many quotes from the Law and the Writings in chapter 12. Also, when you read Paul's commands to respect secular authorities, keep in mind who ruled the world in his day. Not only was the Roman Empire the very antithesis of a Christian government, the emperor was the brutal Nero. If Paul could command believers to respect and obey Nero's government, what does that say about how we should act toward those in power in our nation regardless of their political affiliation?

As you read, underline all the commands Paul gives in these chapters. Count those that deal with interpersonal relationships between believers. Although chapter 16 is primarily personal greetings from Paul to specific people, you will still find some instructions regarding getting along with one another within the church. Compare the number of commands you just counted to Paul's commands for other areas of conduct for believers. What does this say about the importance of this issue to God?

First Corinthians

Simply put, the church in Corinth had problems. Paul started the work there during his second missionary journey. The city itself was a major commercial and cultural center. Corinth served as a bustling seaport, with all the worst that can bring. The city was known for its deviant sexual practices. All sorts of pagan shrines to various gods could be found everywhere. The people who lived there took great pride in their city. They adorned it with intricate artwork. Not only did the city have a strong port, it also sat at the main crossroads of two major highways. This led the people to have an open mind to anything and everything, since they saw anything and everything come through town at least once. Corinth also prided itself on its commercial prowess. While less sophisticated than some other major Roman cities, it was nonetheless prosperous and proud.

Not long after Paul left Corinth, problems began to emerge in the church. Almost every conceivable worst-case scenario played itself out. From gross sexual sin, to members suing one another on a regular basis, to fighting and factions, it was as dysfunctional as a church could possibly be. As the problems grew, a delegation went to see Paul. They carried at least one letter outlining the trouble and asking for help. First Corinthians is Paul's response. As you read, it will seem as though Paul jumps from topic to topic, not bothering to tie them together. He does this because he is going down the list of problems presented by the Corinthians' letter, answering each question through the inspiration of the Holy Spirit.

1 Corinthians 1–2

You would think a church so messed up would receive a harsh response. Yet when Paul writes to the church in Corinth, he doesn't chide them. Instead, his letter opens with a gentle, pastoral tone. Over and over he reminds them he is their spiritual father. He praises them for what they do right, and he confronts head-on the things they shouldn't be doing.

Although the tone is gentle, Paul doesn't let the problems in the church slide. At the root of everything, these people took great pride in themselves and their learning. They believed themselves to be enlightened. Paul confronts their pride with the foolishness of God, which shines through the mystery of Christ crucified.

1 Corinthians 3–5

Paul commands the church to kick a man out of the church, turning him over to Satan so that "his sinful nature will be destroyed" (5:5). This means the full effects of the man's sin will fall down on his head. Paul wants this man to experience all of the consequences of his actions. He isn't being cruel. Remember, God built consequences into action as a way of getting our attention to bring us back to him. Shielding people from the negative results of their sin doesn't do them any favors. Instead, it simply lets them continue to live in a way that cuts them off from fellowship with Christ, while telling the world Christianity is a sham. Tolerating behavior even unbelievers know is wrong doesn't make the gospel more attractive. Instead, it turns people away from the claims of Christ.

1 Corinthians 6–7

To understand Paul's teaching on marriage in chapter 7, you need to keep a couple of things in mind. First, Corinth was awash in sexual immorality. People in the ancient world used the name "Corinth" as an adjective for sexual sin in much the same way we use the name "Sodom." Even without the Internet or cable television, these practices were paraded around in full view. Religious prostitution, where people committed sexual acts in the name of worship, only made the situation worse. The Christians who lived in the city found this culture pressing up against them at every turn.

Second, because of the gross sexual abuses, some Greek philosophers concluded that all sexual activity was bad, even within marriage. They taught that truly enlightened people should abstain from all sexual intimacy. This confused married couples in the church. They wondered if the perversion of God's gift of sexuality that surrounded them meant they too should be celibate even though they were married. Paul answers these questions in 7:3-5.

Finally, some crisis that Paul doesn't describe enveloped the church. The crisis came from external forces, not internal. Apparently some difficult days for the church lay ahead. Paul may have anticipated extreme persecution that sprang up periodically throughout the first century. The Romans alternated between tolerating Christians and trying to exterminate them, depending upon the whims of the emperor. When Rome burned fewer than ten years after Paul wrote this letter, the emperor Nero blamed Christians. Paul himself died in the subsequent storm of persecution. This crisis mode explains why Paul seems to advise believers not to marry. We find this teaching from Paul in 1 Corinthians alone. His other letters lift marriage up as honorable and desirable.

1 Corinthians 8–9

Many of the meat markets in Corinth were connected to the local shrines of the various gods and goddesses. The believers in the church wondered if by eating this meat they were endorsing idols or participating in their worship. Paul's doesn't give a simple yes-or-no answer. His response is a guide to us on gray matters. On the one hand, we have freedom in Christ. On the other, we must always watch to see how our actions affect other believers, some of whom have weaker consciences. What modern parallels do you see to the Corinthian question of meat sacrificed to idols?

1 Corinthians 10–11

Verses 11:1-16 are confusing. Why don't women in churches today wear head coverings when they pray or speak or sing publicly? The entire passage can't be passed over as something unique to the Corinthian culture. Paul mentions the angels as part of his reasoning for saying what he does. One point is clear: Within the church, submission to authority needs to be visible. For a woman to play a prominent role in public worship without a clear deference to her husband's authority brings disgrace on both of them. Paul says she might as well have her head shaved. (In Corinth the only women with short hair were prostitutes, and the only men with long hair were male prostitutes.) See also Ephesians 5 and 6.

Submitting to someone's authority doesn't indicate inferiority, nor does occupying a position of authority indicate superiority or give license to exploit. Rather, God created authority to establish order. In the home, God gives the husband the responsibilities of leadership. Wives are to submit to their husbands as to Christ, while husbands are to love their wives with Christlike sacrifice (Ephesians 5:22-30). When men and women play public roles in the church's worship, they need to show that they live according to this model. A man who neglects his wife shouldn't play a prominent role in the church (1 Timothy 3:2) any more than a woman who refuses to submit to her husband should pray or prophesy. We live in a culture that rejects authority and responsibility and regards these instructions as archaic and ridiculous. That doesn't change the fact that God put them in his Word.

1 Corinthians 12–14

Chapters 12–14 form one unit that focuses on the use of spiritual gifts within the church. The list of gifts isn't comprehensive. See Romans 12:6-8 and Ephesians 4:11-13 for other gifts. At its simplest level, a spiritual gift is a special ability God's Spirit gives each of us with which we can serve him and help the church fulfill its calling. Some are more visible than others. Notice how Paul says those that seem weaker or less important are really the most necessary (12:22). All the gifts are important. Together they enable the church to fully function.

While we usually focus on the list of gifts in 12:8-11 and wonder which we might possess, Paul points to something else as most important. When it comes to these special abilities, we must remember four things. First, we must use these gifts to serve the entire body of Christ, not ourselves. Second, the gifts mean nothing if not used with love. Chapter 13, the love chapter, needs to be understood in the larger context of all three chapters. Third, we should seek the gifts that will make Christ known to unbelievers. We are his ambassadors on earth. Using the gifts he gives in the right way will make him known to the world. And finally, when we meet together, we should do everything in an orderly fashion. The Spirit doesn't breed chaos or confusion. The use of spiritual gifts in a disorderly or chaotic manner is not of God.

1 Corinthians 15–16

The final problem Paul addresses deals with the resurrection. Apparently some false teachers taught the dead wouldn't be raised. This goes to the heart of the gospel. If the dead don't rise, then Jesus stayed dead, and our faith is useless. Chapter 15 brings us back to the centrality of the cross and the empty tomb. Our entire hope hinges on Jesus' rising from the dead. If he stayed dead, Christianity is a sham and should become extinct. We believe and follow Christ not because doing so is helpful, but because the gospel is true. If it weren't true, if Jesus didn't rise, it shouldn't be believed, because doing so would be to believe a lie.

Second Corinthians

Paul wrote 2 Corinthians from the province of Macedonia somewhere around AD 56 or 57, about eighteen months after writing 1 Corinthians. He focuses his attention on refuting the false teachers who invaded the church and attacked him personally. These attacks prompted Paul, by the inspiration of the Holy Spirit, to defend his credentials as an apostle. Paul suffered daily in a variety of ways. The implications are clear. If you and I want to serve God in a way that will yield eternal results, we will also suffer. There is no other way. The stakes are too high and the Enemy is too determined for the road of serving God to be easy. The Corinthians were eager to use their spiritual gifts. Little did they realize that doing so would plant them next to Paul on the trail of hardships. And the same will hold true for each of us.

Second Corinthians is an eyes-wide-open book. It is indispensable reading for everyone who wants to make an eternal difference in others' lives.

2 Corinthians 1–2

Shortly after writing 1 Corinthians, Paul went back to the city for a second visit (the first being the time he spent there starting the church). His trip was less than pleasant. In 2 Corinthians 2:1, he calls it a "painful visit." Apparently he found the situation to be worse than he feared. Not only had the church split into factions (1 Corinthians 1:10-13), but a group of false teachers had also arrived on the scene. They vehemently opposed Paul, questioning his credentials for ministry and harshly criticizing his leadership style. This group of teachers was similar to those who plagued the Galatians. They lifted up the Law and tried to convince these new Gentile believers that they too had to do everything Moses wrote.

After Paul's visit, he fired off a scalding letter. He calls it painful to write, a letter he covered with tears (2 Corinthians 2:4). Although he didn't want to hurt these people into whom he had poured so much of himself, he felt compelled to write because the situation in the church was so serious. And he knew a letter would be better than another visit. We don't know exactly what Paul said in this lost letter. The Holy Spirit didn't preserve it for us as a part of the Bible.

2 Corinthians 3–4

Second Corinthians 3 contrasts the old covenant God made in the Old Testament with the new covenant found in Christ in the New Testament (in fact, the word "testament" is an older word that means "covenant" or "agreement"). The new covenant doesn't nullify the old. It completes and expands it. The heart of the old covenant was this promise to Abraham: "All the families of the earth will be blessed through you" (Genesis 12:3). When Jesus rose from the dead, he opened the door for the entire human race to be forgiven by God, adopted into his family, and brought into his presence forever and ever. This is God's greatest blessing, and it is made possible only through the "new covenant in [Jesus'] blood" (Luke 22:20, NIV). For more on the new covenant, go to Hebrews 8:1–10:18. Don't pass too quickly over it. This covenant is the practical expression of the change made in our lives the day we received Jesus as our Savior.

2 Corinthians 5–6

Does 5:10 teach salvation by works? After all, it says we will stand before God and receive whatever we deserve for the good or evil we do with our bodies here on earth. Does this mean our good has to outweigh our bad for us to get into heaven? If it did, this passage would contradict the rest of the Bible. Ephesians 2:8-9 makes it clear that no one can be saved by doing good. The only way any person can be made right with God is by God's grace through Jesus. However, every believer will stand before the judgment seat of Christ and give an account for everything he has done (Romans 14:10; 1 Corinthians 3:10-15). Whatever we do for Christ's sake will last, while the rest of our life's work will burn up. We'll receive some sort of reward for the good we do to further God's kingdom. Those who have done nothing and yet are believers in Jesus will still be saved. However, they will stand before Christ empty-handed as we cast all the good we've done at his feet in worship of the One who died for us (Revelation 4:10).

2 Corinthians 7
Most people hate confrontation, especially when it comes to confronting someone over sin in his life. Yet that's exactly what the Bible tells us we must do if we love one another. This chapter shows what can happen when we help one another escape sin's deceptive clutches. Notice the roles of sorrow and guilt. Neither is meant to be a final destination, yet both play important roles in moving us to repentance.

2 Corinthians 8–9
Chapters 8–9 focus on giving. Believers in Jerusalem were suffering for their faith. Many people lost everything when they refused to renounce Jesus. To help them survive, Paul took up a collection from the churches with whom he worked throughout Macedonia. In today's reading he encourages the

Corinthian church to take part in this offering, something they volunteered to do a year earlier. As you read, you'll find principles for the way we're supposed to give today.

2 Corinthians 10–11

Here Paul gives a passionate defense of his authority as an apostle. Some self-promoting teachers had ridden into town and tried to destroy Paul's credibility. They didn't attack his message or his integrity. Instead, they focused on the way Paul delivered his sermons. In the process they built themselves up with stories of their experiences and revelations. Paul pulls off the gloves and basically says, "If anyone wants to get into a bragging contest, I can win that game." Yet he brags about the kinds of things that make our hair curl in horror. He lists one trial after another. By the end of the list, we wonder how any one man could endure so much, and why he would do it. Second Corinthians 11:30 reveals his motives. If he must brag, he would rather brag about his weaknesses, for God's power is revealed in human weakness.

These two chapters also remind us that just because someone puts on a good show or speaks eloquently doesn't necessarily mean he is from God. Everything we hear, everything we read, everything that purports to be from God, must be measured against the revelation of God's truth, the Bible. Don't judge by appearances (2 Corinthians 10:7) or believe everything you're told (11:4). Practice diligent discernment.

2 Corinthians 12–13

What was Paul's thorn in the flesh? No one knows. Some think it must have been a physical ailment, such as bad eyesight. Given all he'd been through (2 Corinthians 11), he probably lived with all sorts of physical problems. Others think the thorn was an unruly church member, some person who went out of his or her way to make Paul's life miserable. This interpretation is likely, because the thorn was a "messenger of Satan." In the rest of his letters, Paul never uses the word *messenger* to refer to anything other than a person or angel. Like physical ailments, Paul didn't have a shortage of people who wanted to destroy his ministry. The unnamed people in chapter 11 fit that description. He lists some people by name in 2 Timothy, any of whom might have qualified as a messenger of Satan.

What or who the thorn may have been was far less important than its purpose. God gave Paul this trouble and refused to take it away as a way of making him rely on God's grace every day. Paul had seen so much and done so much that he could have easily fallen into spiritual pride. His ministry was too important to God for him to let that happen. Therefore, the Lord allowed Paul's life to become harder, not easier, as an expression of his love and concern. God built this thorn into his life in order that he might continually rely on the power of the Holy Spirit instead of his own strength.

Galatians

Paul writes Galatians to counter legalism. Most of the believers in Galatia (south central Turkey) are Gentiles, that is, non-Jews. They knew little of the Old Testament before coming to Christ through Paul's preaching. However, Paul has moved on to another region, and some Jewish believers have come from Jerusalem and convinced the Christians in Galatia that Paul told them only part of the story. The proper response to faith in Christ, they say, is to follow the Old Testament Law. After all, the Law came first. And the converts in Galatia believe them. The trouble is that to keep the Jewish Law, they have to stop eating with their Gentile families and neighbors, and they have to undergo circumcision, which their culture sees as bodily mutilation. The gospel ceases to be Christ and becomes Christ plus the Jewish subculture.

Paul's letter to the Galatians uses harsh language to show them how blind they've become. Keeping the Law won't make anyone right with God. If it could, Christ wouldn't have died. Whenever the gospel becomes Christ plus the rules of a subculture, it ceases to be the gospel.

As Paul writes, he answers the key questions regarding the relationships between law and grace, and faith and works. The book of James was written around the same time and addresses the same problem from a different angle. Paul faces legalism in Galatia, while James confronts believers who use their faith as an excuse for spiritual laziness. Since Christ did it all, they reason, they can ignore all the commands in the Bible and do nothing at all. The two extremes are equally wrong.

Galatians 1–3

Galatians is the oldest of Paul's letters that we have in the Bible. Paul wrote it from the city of Antioch around the same time James wrote the book that bears his name, between AD 45 and 50, shortly before the large meeting of church leaders described in Acts 15.

Paul's tone in Galatians sounds harsher than in any other letter. He doesn't sugarcoat his words. If you listen closely, you can almost hear him yelling at these people who think they need to add cultural rules to the finished work of Christ. He also gives us insight into the true nature of legalism. When people try to impose a set of rules on believers, they never say such efforts will get a person into heaven. Instead, they say following rules like "don't listen to rock music, don't get tattoos, and don't get body piercings" show that a person is really serious about following Jesus. Rules like no dancing and no cards crop up in each generation, as believers try to nail down how a good Christian should behave. What's so wrong with that?

According to Galatians, everything. Galatians 3:3 gets to the heart of the problem: "Have you lost your senses? After starting your Christian lives in the Spirit, why are you now trying to become perfect by your own human effort?" As followers of Christ, we are to live by faith and the transforming power of the Spirit from beginning to end (Romans 1:17). And that's the problem with trying to live out the Christian life through a system of rules. We're supposed to follow Christ by faith. Listening only to Christian music and avoiding getting tattoos doesn't take faith. These rules may help us look like Christians, but they're useless substitutes for what the Holy Spirit wants to do in us: make us as loving, joyful, and patient as Jesus is. Our faith must grow every day for us to be able to see an invisible God and place our feet in his footprints.

Galatians 4–6

Galatians 5:4 can be abused if removed from the overall context of the entire book of Galatians. The last phrase of the verse says, "You have fallen away from God's grace." Through the years this phrase has come to be used to describe losing one's salvation. But is that what Paul is talking about? Usually we think of someone who has lost his salvation as someone who once confessed faith in Christ but goes back to a lifestyle of sin. Yet Paul uses the phrase to describe people who once depended on God's grace but are now trying to perfect their salvation by keeping a list of rules. Galatians 5:4 doesn't refer to people who've gone back to a lifestyle of sex, drugs, and rock 'n' roll, but to people who don't dance and don't chew and don't date girls who do. Those who have been cut off from Christ and have fallen from grace aren't those who live decadent lifestyles, but those who are the most rigid, those most religious in a mechanical sense, the most legalistic.

So what does 5:4 mean? When we try to justify ourselves by keeping the law, we move from the realm of God's grace—where forgiveness is free and the Holy Spirit empowers us to live for Christ—to a realm where we have to keep every law God ever wrote. Can anyone keep all of the law all of the time? Absolutely not. That's the purpose of the law, to show us our utter sinfulness and our need for God's grace. Legalism tries to convince us we don't need grace, we just need to work a little harder. Read Romans 7 for Paul's commentary on how successful this strategy will ultimately be.

Ephesians

No single church plays a more prominent role in the New Testament than the church in Ephesus. Paul, Timothy, and John all guided the church over the course of thirty years. The city and its inhabitants are mentioned more than twenty times in six New Testament books. The city was the fourth largest in the world in Paul's day, with a population estimated at 250,000. The capital of Asia Minor (modern Turkey), Ephesus was a political, religious, and commercial center. The major temple for the goddess Artemis was built there in 250 BC and was one of the seven wonders of the ancient world.

Paul stopped briefly in Ephesus during his second missionary journey, and then returned to spend three years there during his third mission trip. Paul wrote the book of Ephesians—along with Philippians, Colossians, and Philemon—a few years later while a prisoner in Rome. The letter lacks many of the personal touches we find in 1 and 2 Corinthians and some of his other letters. Most likely Paul meant for this letter to go beyond the one church in Ephesus. In the time since Paul left, the church had started other churches in the surrounding area. Copies of this letter were to be passed around among all the churches, not just the one Paul started in the city.

Ephesians 1–3

Ephesians is much like Romans in that both give grand overviews of the central truths of Christianity. Whereas Romans focuses on the gospel, Ephesians looks at God's plan for the world and our part in it. We find God working from eternity past to eternity future to accomplish his secret plan that has now been revealed in Christ. You and I have been included in this plan even though we were once separated from God because of our sin. God's grace took care of that. Now God has joined us together, both Jews and Gentiles, as a holy temple where God's Spirit resides. As you read, notice how often Paul refers to God's secret plan, the mystery that has now been revealed. Why was this plan a mystery? What makes this such a radical message both in Paul's day and our own?

Ephesians 4–6

Ephesians 4:1–5:20 tells us how to conduct ourselves in this world. The first three chapters show us God's awesome plan. Now we see how to live in response to what God is doing. Pay close attention to both the positive and negative commands. Trying to go forward with Jesus while dragging along our favorite sins won't work. Yet walking with Christ means more than letting go of old vices. A walk worthy of our calling is a constant contrast between who we once were and who we have become in Christ.

Verses 5:21–6:9 explore how God's grace changes our human relationships. Paul touches on three areas: marriage, parenting, and work. You will find he is an equal-opportunity offender. We can all find something we don't like in each of these three areas, whether the commands concern submission, obedience, or service. This passage makes it clear that Christianity has never been a "what's in this for me?" religion. The last set of commands refers to slaves and their masters. Do you find Paul's approach to slavery surprising? Why? What underlying principle is at work here?

The final section of the book deals with spiritual warfare and the weapons God gives us to defeat the Enemy. Compare this list with 1 Thessalonians 5:8. Before Paul talks about the armor and weapons at our disposal, he gives us insight into the true nature of the Enemy we face. As you read 6:10-12, ask yourself what these verses say about the moral challenges you encounter.

Philippians

Philippi has the distinction of being the first place in Europe where Paul went with the gospel. It was also the place where Paul and Silas were arrested, beaten, jailed, and bound in leg stocks. Read how they reacted and the miracle God worked through an earthquake in Acts 16:22-34. Paul felt a special bond with the people in this church because of their shared suffering. Through the years the church continued to support Paul. In fact, he wrote this letter in response to a financial gift they sent him while he was in prison in Rome. Because of Paul's close relationship with them, he warns them of false teachers who might sneak into their midst and pervert the gospel. This is a common theme in most of Paul's letters, because bad theology is one of Satan's favorite weapons against Christ's church.

Philippians 1–2

Philippians stands out as one of the Bible's most upbeat, joy-filled books. Even though Paul doesn't know if he will live or die, he urges these believers to rejoice always. Not even the prospect of execution can dampen Paul's spirits. He sees this as a difficult choice. If the Romans put him to death, he gets to go home to heaven and be with Christ. However, if they turn him loose, he will be able to continue the work God gave him to do. The fact that Paul found this to be such a difficult dilemma shows us the attitude we should have. The world is not our home. Our real home is in heaven in the presence of God. We should now live like it.

Pay particular attention to 2:1-11. These verses mark one of the most complete explanations of what Jesus did when he took on flesh and came to earth. Note also how we are to follow his example. This passage, sometimes referred to as the *kenosis* passage (from the Greek word for "empty"), is both beautiful and challenging. It describes in a nutshell the greatness of God's love and the hope he gives us in his Son.

Philippians 3–4

Calling the false teachers "dogs" is more of an insult than our Western minds might imagine. The Jews found dogs to be disgusting, vile creatures. This was the ultimate insult and richly deserved. Legalism takes away from the cross and causes us to put our confidence in ourselves rather than in Christ alone. Paul goes on to share part of his own story to show that if anyone should have confidence in himself, it is he. As you read, pay close attention to 3:7-11. How does your life need to change in light of what you just read?

In the midst of this incredible book, we find 4:2, a verse two people probably wish had not been written. How would you like to be Euodia or Syntyche, two women who are now forever remembered for how they couldn't get along? Keep that in mind as you read further admonitions to rejoice always, pray without ceasing, and be content with whatever God gives you.

Colossians

Colossae was a small village on the south bank of the Lycus River in the interior of Asia Minor (modern Turkey). A major highway once ran through the city, but the road shifted north to the towns of Hierapolis and Laodicea. When the highway left, so did the source of commerce. By Paul's day, the city was well on its way to becoming a ghost town with an ever-shrinking population. In fact, a short time after Paul wrote this letter, the town ceased to exist when a huge earthquake struck the region. The fact that the Holy Spirit led Paul to write to a church in such a backwater village gives us insight into the way God sees the world. Size doesn't matter to him. Little churches in small towns no one ever notices matter just as much to him as do megachurches in major metropolitan areas.

Paul had never been to Colossae. Most likely the church had been started by one of his associates, a man named Epaphras. Paul felt compelled to write when Epaphras came to him and told him of false teaching sweeping through the church. This teaching combined elements of Jewish rituals and holy days, Greek philosophy and asceticism, and quasi-Christianity that didn't deny Christ but rather dethroned him. Parts of this teaching were an early form of what later came to be known as Gnosticism (from the Greek word for "knowledge"), which taught that all physical matter was evil, that minor deities mediated between God and people, and that salvation comes through knowledge. Gnostics didn't believe Jesus was fully God and fully human. This heresy was in its embryonic form when Paul wrote this letter.

Colossians 1–2

The emergence of an early heresy akin to Gnosticism explains why Paul places so much emphasis on the person and work of Christ in the first chapter. Here we find Jesus is fully God, yet he was also fully human. Paul goes on to warn the church not to be taken in by "empty philosophy and high-sounding nonsense that come from human thinking and from the evil powers of this world, and not from Christ" (2:8). The truths found in this book demonstrate God's foresight. He framed the answers to one of the first heresies even before it got off the ground. This also shows us our Enemy's tactics. He attacks from the outside through persecution and trials, but also from the inside through false teachers who sound good but whose message doesn't stand up to God's revealed truth as found in his Word.

Colossians 3–4

The "enlightened" teachers who'd descended on Colossae drew a sharp line between the body and the spirit. The body was evil. Because of this, they taught a strict asceticism designed to deny the flesh what it craved—rules like: Don't eat. Don't touch. Don't get near that. That's the only way to keep this evil flesh under control, they taught. These same ideas can be found today in groups that teach that caffeine is evil and television sets have no place in a Christian home. You need a great deal of discipline and devotion to the rules to keep them. But, as Paul goes on to teach in chapters 3–4, they have no value when it comes to living a life that pleases God.

First and Second Thessalonians

Paul wrote 1 and 2 Thessalonians to encourage those who suffered for their faith. Neither letter tells us why we must suffer for Christ. It's as though Paul assumes we know the reason. Instead, the letters encourage us to keep hanging on to Christ. We wonder how long God will let our pain continue. Reading these two letters, we know an end is in sight. But God promises to do more than end our suffering. His Son will soon come back for us. In that moment, as we melt into his arms, we will find the temporary afflictions we suffer in this life can't compare to the joy that will never end.

The subject of suffering rounds out the first set of obstacles each of us faces when we decide to follow Christ. Along with trying to find the balance between faith and works, law and grace, we must also learn that the path of faith isn't easy to travel. Trials await every believer. First and Second Thessalonians help prepare us for the journey.

1 Thessalonians 1–3

When Paul first preached the good news about Jesus in the city of Thessalonica, the Jews in the city stirred up a riot against him (Acts 17:1-9). Several of the new believers were attacked and arrested, including a man named Jason who let Paul stay in his home. Paul and his traveling companions had to leave the city, because their presence created a near-riot situation. Shortly after leaving, Paul penned this letter (around AD 51) from Corinth, farther south in Greece. You can hear his deep love and concern for the church in Thessalonica in the first three chapters. Paul makes so many personal references, we know we're reading someone else's mail.

These first three chapters also show one of the great paradoxes of Christianity. Faithfulness to Christ often leads to hardships and pain, yet believers' suffering causes news about Jesus to spread faster and farther. When we suffer patiently for Christ, we make the gospel more attractive to others. Our faithfulness also silences the skeptics and turns the truth of Christ into a spotlight that pierces the darkness.

1 Thessalonians 4–5

The tone of the letter changes in the last two chapters. Paul moves from expressing his love to reminding his readers how they should love one another. These two chapters are filled with commands. Most involve our relationships with one another. All show how facing suffering only increases the need for genuine Christianity. Note how 4:12 says we can earn the respect of unbelievers and thus make the gospel more attractive to them. Verses 5:16-18 tell us God's will for our lives. Together, these two chapters are incredibly practical—and challenging.

Verses 4:13-18 are the most popular verses in either letter to the Thessalonians. They express our great hope and confidence. Because we know Jesus will return someday soon, we need not fear anything this world throws at us. However, as you read, make note of what these verses and those that follow don't say. They lack details about *when* Christ will return. Paul doesn't say a word about clues to help us construct a timetable. Instead, he focuses on the fact that Christ will return and the hope this assurance gives us. Chapter 5 tells us how we should live in light of the hope that Jesus will come back.

2 Thessalonians

The Bible doesn't give many details about Christ's Second Coming. Because of this, many people tend to reach faulty conclusions about the matter. That's exactly what happened after the church in Thessalonica received Paul's first letter. Reading his encouragement based on the hope of Jesus' soon return, people made two equally wrong assumptions. Some false teachers said the Second Coming had already taken place and the people left in the church had missed it. Others assumed that since Jesus would return soon, they should just sit back and wait for it to happen. They quit their jobs and stopped providing for their families. Why bother with something as trivial as money when Jesus would come back any day?

Paul wrote a second letter a few months after the first to address both of these questions. It too was written from Corinth in AD 51 or 52. The second letter doesn't give any timetables or surefire signs to let everyone know when the Second Coming would occur. Paul instead reminds them of the single most important thing they can do to prepare for Christ's return: live faithfully for him.

To counter the idea that the Second Coming has already taken place, Paul reminds us of one sign that will precede Christ's return: the rise of the man of lawlessness. Also known as the Antichrist and the Beast, this man of lawlessness will fool the world with satanically empowered miracles. Revelation 13 also talks about him. Paul gives no clues as to when this person will arise. His point isn't to give us information but to remind us that evil will grow more and more intense until the end of time. Therefore, we shouldn't be surprised when it rears its ugly head, or when it opposes us as we try to please God. We live in a fallen world that hates Jesus. It hates those who love him. When this hatred lands in our laps, why are we shocked?

The Pastoral Letters

Three of Paul's letters stand apart because they aren't written to churches as a whole but to a church leader. First and Second Timothy and Titus are known as the pastoral letters, because Timothy and Titus served as pastors of churches. These men were two of Paul's closest companions. He writes to encourage them to stand firm against false teachers and not to get bogged down in the foolish arguments such teachers love to launch. The pastoral letters also emphasize order. Jesus never meant for his church to be chaotic. Instead, in both their worship and their leadership, the churches need a basic structure. Chaos confuses, order allows growth. However, the structure Paul prescribes is not so overwhelming that it would crush the moving of the Spirit. He doesn't lay down a huge list of rules. His instructions stand out for their brevity, something many churches today should emulate.

1 Timothy 1–3

Paul met Timothy in Lystra during his second missionary journey and immediately saw the leadership potential in him. Timothy's mother was a Jew and a believer, his father a Greek. His father is never referred to as a Christian. All the believers in Lystra and Iconium spoke highly of Timothy, so Paul invited him to join his team. Before long, Paul sent Timothy to churches as his representative to help put things in order or left him behind after preaching the gospel in an area to strengthen new believers until they were firmly established. Paul even includes Timothy with himself in the initial greetings in six of the New Testament letters.

At some point, Paul sent Timothy to Ephesus for extended ministry. Since he was much younger than Paul, some people in the church discounted Timothy's leadership ability. Paul encourages his young apprentice to silence those critics by proving himself to be a strong example of faith, love, and purity. Paul led by example, and he encourages Timothy to do the same. He also gives him instructions for appointing leaders. Strong, godly leadership allows churches to reach their full potential in Christ.

In chapter 3, Paul uses the term "elder" to refer to the primary leadership of the church. The term also refers to pastors, a word that itself means "shepherd." A third term, "overseer" (KJV: "bishop"), refers to the same leadership position.

The second term Paul uses in 1 Timothy 3, "deacons," is less a translation and more a transliteration. The Greek word *diakonos* means "servant, one who serves, a helper." When Paul talks about deacons in 1 Timothy 3, he isn't talking about a second office of authority within the church. Rather, he tells us what is required of those who would be servant leaders within the church. The Message renders 3:8 as, "The same goes for those who want to be servants in the church." Verse 11 describes women who serve in the church, rather than the wives of deacons.

1 Timothy 4–6

These chapters break down some of the legalistic myths many groups try to place upon churches. There are those who say pastors should not be paid, that giving them money compromises the integrity of their work. What does Paul tell Timothy about this idea? Others say Christians should never consume alcohol in any form. While the Bible makes it clear that getting drunk is wrong (Romans 13:13; 1 Corinthians 5:11; Ephesians 5:18), it doesn't prohibit drinking wine as a beverage. Notice what 5:23 says about this. Also notice the adjective Paul uses with the word "wine." Still, remember Paul's words to the church in Rome about eating and drinking (Romans 14:1-23). We need to be very careful to make sure our freedom in Christ doesn't cause others to stumble.

The third myth these chapters debunk is the myth of nonconfrontation. Many, many believers have the mistaken idea that seeking unity and love within the community means never confronting people over perceived errors. They think confronting disagreements is always judgmental. What does Paul tell Timothy about such ideas? Remember as well Jesus' example. After reading the Gospels, could you honestly say he avoided all confrontations?

2 Timothy

Last words always carry extra weight. Second Timothy is Paul's final message before being put to death. He wrote this letter from a Roman jail around AD 66 or 67. Most likely this was Paul's second time to land in jail in Rome. His first imprisonment came when the Jewish leaders in Jerusalem tried to put him to death. He had to appeal to Caesar to escape the situation alive. We know about this imprisonment thanks to Luke's details in Acts. Most scholars believe Paul was released after his appeal was heard, traveled again for a while, but was then rearrested. In AD 64, Emperor Nero blamed Christians for a massive fire in Rome. He slaughtered dozens of Christians immediately and swept others up in arrests. Paul was probably among this latter group. He wrote this final letter while awaiting his sentencing and execution.

Paul wrote these last words to an individual rather than a church. Pay close attention to the concerns he raises. Also note how he viewed his life and the fate that awaited him. What do these words tell you about your priorities?

Titus

Titus was, like Timothy, one of Paul's younger assistants. He too was entrusted with strengthening and bringing order to churches. Although we don't find any details about Titus in Acts, we know he accompanied Paul on his later journeys. At times Paul sent him to a city as his representative. In 2 Corinthians we learn Paul sent Titus to Corinth to encourage the church as they took up a special offering to help believers in Jerusalem.

Paul wrote to Titus around AD 64 while Titus was working with churches on the island of Crete. Paul left Titus on Crete to appoint leadership for the churches in each town and to stop false teaching by promoting sound teaching. Although much shorter than 1 Timothy, this letter is very practical. Notice how right beliefs work their way out in everyday life.

Philemon

Philemon is the shortest of Paul's letters and the most personal. It is addressed to an individual, a believer in Colossae named Philemon, regarding his runaway slave, Onesimus. When Onesimus escaped, he apparently stole something, but Paul doesn't say what. Paul met the runaway while in prison and led him to Christ. The one-time fugitive who hadn't been much use to anyone then became a valued coworker of Paul. In fact, along with Tychicus, Onesimus delivered the letter to the Colossians.

This letter, then, is Paul's appeal for forgiveness and reconciliation between the fugitive thief and his master, Philemon. Paul doesn't ask Philemon to set Onesimus free, but he does ask him to see him through the lens of God's grace. Instead of seeing him as a slave who could legally be executed for running away, Philemon should regard him as a brother in Christ. As for any outstanding debts, Paul says he will repay them himself.

This short book shows us the power of God's grace and the process of reconciliation. In Christ, labels about social class and ethnicity no longer matter. All that matters is Christ who lives within us. And if he lives within us, we must live like it, even when that demands that we forgive those from whom we would rather exact a little revenge.

Hebrews

This book is called Hebrews because it appears to be written to an audience of Jewish believers. We can't make a firm pronouncement about the audience, because unlike the other letters of the New Testament, Hebrews doesn't say to whom it was written. Nor does it say who wrote it or when. Since the author speaks of the sacrificial system and the temple as though they are still intact, the book was probably written before the Romans destroyed Jerusalem in AD 70. Most likely the unknown author penned these words sometime in the mid-60s, around the same time Peter wrote the first of his two letters and Paul wrote 1 Timothy and Titus.

That the book was intended for a congregation of Jewish believers seems clear. From beginning to end, Hebrews assumes the readers know the Old Testament, with references to Moses, Melchizedek, and the sacrificial system. The original readers of this letter were raised on the Old Testament, with its regular feasts and sacrifices. They grew up looking forward to the day the Messiah would come and bring back the glory the Jews once enjoyed. When they came to Christ, they thought they had found the One for whom they'd waited so long. But with time, doubt crept in. They paid a heavy price for believing in Jesus. From the day they first believed, they'd endured public ridicule, beatings, and imprisonment. After a while, the pain wore them down. They had to ask themselves, *Is this worth it? If Jesus is the Messiah, why doesn't he do something to stop this?*

That is why the writer takes us back through the Old Testament. His point is not to show us how Jesus is better than everything that came before, but that he is the fulfillment of it all. All of history up to Christ's coming moved toward his coming. The Old Testament story all comes together in the cross and the Resurrection. How could anyone go back when God has moved forward?

Hebrews 1–2

Jesus is more than a man and more than an angel. He is God in human flesh. The first three verses make eight statements about who Jesus is. How do these, when taken together, change your understanding of Jesus? Notice also how the Father tells all the angels to worship the Son. Compare this to the first commandment in Exodus 20:3. If God alone is to be worshiped, and all the angels are told to worship the Son, the Son of God must be—what? Chapter 1 does more than show Jesus' superiority to the angels. It also shows his true nature and affirms the doctrine of the Trinity.

Hebrews 2:1-4 contains the first of five warning passages in Hebrews. It warns that if people in the Old Testament were punished for not obeying the message God communicated through the angels, how much more so should we listen to his final word spoken through his Son? As you read the rest of the chapter, think about how it sounded to people suffering for the name of Jesus. He is the One the angels worship, yet he took on flesh and blood because we are made of flesh and blood. Herein lies the great mystery: Why would God take on flesh and dwell among us?

Hebrews 3–5

No one ranked higher in Jewish eyes than Moses. He was the lawgiver, the greatest prophet who led the people out of slavery in Egypt and took them to the doorstep of the Promised Land. Yet compared with Jesus, Moses is like a servant compared with the boss. By saying Moses is Jesus' servant, the writer implies that the Law points toward the Son. Once the Son arrives, the lawgiver steps into the background. God sent Moses and the Law to lead us to Christ. Once we arrive at our destination, would we want to go back to the journey?

The comparison with Moses comes with a warning. Those who didn't listen to Moses died in the wilderness, never entering into God's rest (see Numbers 14). Now that One greater than Moses has arrived, how much more do we need to listen to and act on what he says? Notice the progression within the book. The author is speaking to people contemplating going back to their old ways of life. They don't plan on becoming pagans. Instead, they want to go back to the faith of their fathers, back to a Judaism still waiting for the Messiah. Yet, if someone greater than Moses has arrived, how can they go back now?

These chapters also address the priesthood. Old Testament priests represented the people to God. They offered sacrifices on their behalf and asked God to show them mercy. Jesus has now come as the greatest of all priests who intercedes for us to God and offers himself as a sacrifice. For more on Melchizedek, see Genesis 14.

Hebrews 6–8

What's the big deal about Melchizedek? This book's comparison of Jesus with Melchizedek is actually longer than the narrative about him in Genesis 14. Why is this man about whom we know so little so crucial to our understanding of Jesus? The reason lies in that Jesus is our high priest. In the Old Testament, priests came from the tribe of Levi. Jesus was born into the tribe of Judah. He had to be from Judah to qualify as the Messiah. Nearly two thousand years before Christ, Jacob prophesied of

Judah saying, "The scepter will not depart from Judah, nor the ruler's staff from his descendants, until the coming of the one to whom it belongs" (Genesis 49:10). Judah was the tribe of kings beginning with David. Priests, however, came from the tribe of Levi. How then could Jesus be a priest who intercedes on our behalf before the Father? On a human level, Jesus didn't qualify. That's why the writer of Hebrews points back to a time before the Law to the priest-king Abraham himself honored as God's representative: Melchizedek. Jesus' position as our high priest stretches back before the Law was given.

Why does this matter to us? After all, we aren't Jews. Yet this question matters every time we offer up a prayer. We take it for granted that God hears our prayers. However, the Bible says our sin separates us from God. Someone has to intercede on our behalf if we are to be heard. That Someone is Jesus, the Great High Priest. He tore down the barrier that existed between us and God. Now we can enter God's presence because Jesus opens the way.

Hebrews 9–10

Why don't we have to sacrifice a sheep when we sin today? The Jews sacrificed sheep and goats and cows and even pigeons until the Lord made that impossible by taking the temple away from them. (The Romans demolished the temple in AD 70.) These chapters explain the end of the system of animal sacrifices and what Jesus did for us on the cross. After reading these chapters, ask yourself, *What could I add to this?* Cults constantly try to add something else to Jesus' finished work on the cross. What do these two chapters have to say about that?

Chapter 10 contains another warning passage. Jesus offered the ultimate sacrifice for our sins. If we turn our backs on him, not just slipping into an old lifestyle of sin but saying we don't need what he did, what hope could we possibly have? Once again, a stern warning is followed by words of encouragement in 10:32-39.

Hebrews 11
Without faith, it is impossible to please God. But what does faith look like in the real world? Chapter 11 has been called the "Faith Hall of Fame," for it chronicles the faith lives of some of the giants of the Old Testament. However, some of the names will not be familiar to you. Some are even surprising, given their less-than-stellar track record. Again, the inclusion of those we wouldn't immediately put alongside the others on this list is evidence of the power of God's grace.

Hebrews 12–13
Hebrews covers a lot of ground. The tone is at times harsh, but given the stakes for the original readers, it had to be. The book's message is as vital now as it was in AD 64. That is why the book closes with encouragement. Again, keep in mind that those who first received this letter were on the verge of abandoning the faith. They felt frustrated over their suffering. Like the rest of us, they just wanted some peace. These chapters encourage the weary to hold on and trust that God knows what he's doing. Note the role we play in one another's lives in this process. Also listen as Hebrews reminds us of the seriousness of the issues before us. Skeptics try to minimize the importance of questions about God. What do these chapters say about that?

James

James' letter was probably the first book of the New Testament to be written. It addresses a mainly Jewish audience scattered across the ancient Near East. These believers knew the Old Testament Law. They'd grown up with it before finding freedom in Christ. Yet apparently there were those who thought this freedom meant they didn't have to do anything for God. They believed they could simply believe facts about Christ and leave it at that. Since they were free from the Law, the way they lived didn't matter. James writes to counter this false idea and to show how real faith expresses itself in a changed life.

James is the brother of Jesus (Mark 6:3; Galatians 1:19) and the leader of the church in Jerusalem (Acts 12:17; 15:13-29; Galatians 1:18-19). He writes sometime between AD 45 and 50, shortly before the large meeting of all the leaders of the churches recorded in Acts 15. Paul wrote Galatians to a Gentile audience at the same time in response to the same sort of questions. Together the two books answer some of the first questions we face when we become Christians. If all we have to do to be saved is believe, how will our lives change? And how does faith in Christ work with the rest of the Bible with all its instructions for how to live?

James 1–3

Does James 2 contradict the book of Galatians? In Galatians, Paul says we are saved by faith alone apart from works. James says we are not saved by "faith" disconnected from works. If the two contradict one another, how can they both be correct?

James doesn't say keeping the Jewish Law will save anyone (which is the issue Paul addresses in Galatians). Rather, he focuses on what constitutes real faith. Anything that claims to be faith in God but doesn't result in a changed life isn't real. He uses compassion toward the poor as a barometer of the validity of our faith. If we can ignore the physical needs of our brothers and sisters in Christ, how can our faith be real?

James 4–5

The words that come out of our mouths either reveal Christ in our hearts, or they show our faith to be a sham. Yet nothing is harder to control than our tongues. Chapter 4 builds on chapter 3 by showing the results of an uncontrolled tongue. Controlling the tongue is more than a matter of ridding our speech of profanity. How many sins of speech can you spot in James 4? Maybe I shouldn't have asked that question. This chapter isn't a lot of fun to read.

Chapter 5 brings us full circle in the book. If faith without works is dead, how should we act when we see a so-called believer not living his faith? James tells us in the last two verses of the book. These verses weed out the legalist who lives in all of us. Rather than standing back criticizing others while we brag about our own godliness, people with hearts that have been changed by God's grace will constantly reach out to those who've wandered away from the truth. Love has to compel us to act. Without it, our words are hollow.

First and Second Peter

On the day of Pentecost (Acts 2), Peter became the undisputed leader of the early church. However, his status within the church is not matched by his literary output. God included only two of his letters in the New Testament. The first was written from Rome (which Peter referred to symbolically as Babylon in 5:13) around the same time Paul wrote 1 Timothy and Titus. This letter went out to several churches at one time, all of which were spread across the northern half of Asia Minor (modern Turkey). Although Acts doesn't give us any details, Peter spent his life traveling around spreading the gospel, just as Paul did. Most of the people in these churches were probably Gentiles from pagan backgrounds rather than converted Jews.

1 Peter 1–2

Everything Peter says in this letter builds on the address line. He calls believers "God's elect, strangers in the world" (1:1, NIV). He means that because God has chosen you through Jesus Christ, you don't fit in on earth any longer. Your real home is in heaven. Now live like it. Pursue holiness because God is holy. Also, because you don't fit in on earth, life will not be a smooth ride. Suffering, especially suffering for the sake of Jesus, is the new normal for believers. Instead of complaining, Peter says to embrace it and allow it to purify your life. Peter calls suffering a trial and a test. He writes from the unique perspective of one who had failed as many tests as he passed. Yet God never gave up on him, just as he never gives up on us.

1 Peter 3–5

Who are "the spirits in prison"? The words used in the original language indicate that these are fallen angels who were active on the earth before and during the time of Noah. Genesis describes this period of time as the worst of the bad old days. People across the entire world had sunk to such a level that they were beyond help. These fallen angels actively stirred the human race to deeper and deeper depths of depravity. When God destroyed the world through the Flood, he locked away many of the spirits so they could no longer wreak havoc on the earth. When Jesus died and rose again, he went to these spirits and proclaimed his victory on the cross. The word translated "preach" in 1 Peter 3 simply means to proclaim. That's what Jesus did. He didn't give them a second chance. Instead, he showed how all they had worked to accomplish had failed. Jesus declared his victory once and for all.

Does Peter imply we have to be baptized to go to heaven when he says, "This is a picture of baptism, which now saves you"? No. Peter does not mean to imply that the act of being baptized can save anyone. Instead, he points to the meaning behind baptism: "an appeal to God from a good conscience" (3:21). Churches didn't have altar calls two thousand years ago. That innovation came in the late 1800s. In the New Testament, people made their commitment to Christ public through the act of baptism. That's what Peter refers to here.

Finally, what does he mean when he writes, "That is why the Good News was preached even to those who have died—so that although their bodies were punished with death, they could still live in the spirit as God does" (1 Peter 4:6)? Some people try to make this verse say that those in hell can be given another chance at life. If that were the case, hell would be emptied out in a nanosecond. But this interpretation doesn't conform to any other passage in the Bible. The most obvious meaning of this verse is also the simplest. The gospel was preached to people who believed and received Christ as their Savior. They later died, even though Christians in the first century thought Jesus would come back before any of them could die. We know from Paul's two letters to the Thessalonians that some false teachers tried to say that Christians who died before the Second Coming missed out on heaven. First Peter 4:6 makes it clear that is not the case. As followers of Christ, even though our physical bodies may die, we still live, for in Christ, we have eternal life.

2 Peter

Peter wrote this second letter shortly before his death in AD 67. His final words focus on three simple themes. First, we must grow spiritually. We grow by increasing our knowledge of God through both the Bible and experiencing God amid trials. We have to live this knowledge on a daily basis as we put on godliness and love one another.

His second theme warns against false doctrine. Just as false prophets filled Israel during her history, false teachers will infiltrate Christian circles. We must become spiritually mature through the Bible and the crucible of trials in order to see through the lies of false teachers. They surround us today, just as Peter warned. We must exercise discernment before swallowing what some "expert" teaches. Just because he quotes the Bible doesn't necessarily mean he teaches biblical truth.

Finally, Peter tells us to be ready for Christ's return. The day is coming. Scoffers may wonder what is taking him so long, but God's patience is actually an act of his grace. When Jesus does return, this world and everything in it will be consumed by fire. Nothing here will last. Why then should we spend our lives chasing after it as though it were permanent?

First, Second, and Third John

The three letters of John stand out as unique, for they are the only letters in the New Testament written by the author of one of the four Gospels. The difference this makes jumps out from the very beginning as the fourth gospel and these letters parallel one another. The first chapter of John's gospel introduced the good news of Jesus so we might see him for who he truly is and believe in him. The first chapter of 1 John goes back to the good news for those who have believed that we might walk with Jesus in truth. First John 1 says these things are announced and written down so the hearer might "have fellowship with us . . . (and) with the Father and with his Son," and "our joy will be complete." If we believe all we read in the gospel of John, we will experience the fellowship and the joy we find in 1 John.

1 John 1–2

Seven times in the first chapter, John graphically describes the face-to-face encounter he and the other apostles had with God incarnate. All of what follows, every word, every command, every test of the validity of faith, flows from his experience with the Eternal Word made flesh. This explains John's bluntness throughout this letter. He's not offering good advice on how we should live as Christians. Rather, he writes to show how the lives of those who have encountered Jesus Christ in a real and dynamic way should now change. Coming face-to-face with Jesus leaves no room for an anemic, wishy-washy Christianity. Someone on the fringe of the Christian movement may think 1 John is judgmental, but anyone who has personally encountered the same living God will immediately understand that John is absolutely correct when he tells us those who know Christ must walk in the light.

1 John 3–5

Does 1 John 3:4-6 teach that Christians never sin? Not at all. If that were the case, why would John also talk about how eager God is to forgive in 1:9? Chapter 3 speaks of a lifestyle. Those who have been born again will not continue in habitual sin. Their lives will be markedly different from everyone else's. The key characteristic of God's children is love, while children of the Devil continue in a lifestyle of sin. But John doesn't leave any room for warm fuzzy feelings about what love means. As you read, underline all the commands he connects to love. Loving others as God loves us, not just avoiding sin, marks a righteous lifestyle.

2 John and 3 John

These two very brief letters emphasize two of the themes of 1 John: love and believing the truth. In 3 John, love expresses itself in hospitality toward strangers. In 2 John, loving God means holding fast to the truth of his Son. John includes an interesting command in 2 John 10-11. If people come around teaching things that distort the truth of Jesus Christ, we are not to invite them into our homes or encourage them in any way. Doing so makes us a partner in spreading their lies.

Jude

Jude is one of the shortest books of the New Testament. The author was, like James, one of the physical brothers of Jesus. His twenty-five short verses warn us of the dangers of false teachers. The book shares much in common with 2 Peter, both in its tone and subject matter. The closing words of the book mark one of the greatest messages of encouragement found in the Bible.

As you read, you will probably have a couple of "what's he talking about?" moments. Jude quotes two books not found in the Bible. The first, in verse 9, comes from an apocryphal book called the Assumption of Moses, only small portions of which have survived. The second, a long quote in verses 14-15, comes from the Book of Enoch, which was popular among Jews and Christians at that time. By quoting these two books, Jude is not saying either should be considered Scripture. He is simply quoting current literature, much as Paul quotes an Athenian philosopher in Acts 17.

Revelation

Revelation must be approached carefully. Throughout the past nineteen centuries, scholars and commentators have disagreed on even the most basic questions of how to interpret it. This means all of us need to tread lightly as we enter the book. Any conclusions drawn from it about how the future will unfold should always come with the caveat, "But of course, I may be wrong."

Revelation 1–3

Revelation stands apart from the other books in the New Testament not only because of its content, but also for how it came about. The entire book is a collection of visions revealed to John one Sunday while he was exiled on the island of Patmos. Most scholars believe John penned this book late in the first century. By this point he was probably the last surviving member of the original twelve disciples.

These visions have a very clear purpose from God. They weren't given to stoke our curiosity or to give us clues about when the Second Coming may occur. God gave John these visions for him to pass on to the believers in seven specific churches. As you read them, notice how practical the opening seven letters to the seven churches are. These set the tone for the rest of the book. The rest of the visions need to be understood in light of these seven messages.

Revelation 4–7

Chapters 4–5 take place in heaven. In them we learn the business of heaven. Everything that takes place there revolves around worship. The twenty-four thrones and the twenty-four elders in chapter 4 represent the twelve tribes of Israel and the twelve apostles, that is, both Israel and the church. All believers from all time gather around God's throne and sing his praises. Compare the song of 4:8 with Isaiah 6. The scroll in 5:1 represents all of human history. God holds it in his hand to show he is the Lord over history. Events on earth are not random. Whatever may happen, God is in control. The fact that only the Lamb of God (the crucified and risen Lord Jesus Christ) can take the scroll and break its seals shows that Christ isn't a sidelight to history, but its central figure.

Chapter 6 closely parallels Matthew 24, where Jesus describes the events that will take place before his return. While conditions may get worse at the end of days, these disasters have been occurring throughout history as we await Jesus' return. The world won't get better and better through human progress and enlightenment. Instead, we will continually see wars, economic upheavals, disease, attacks against the gospel, and earthquakes, just as we have for two thousand years.

The 144,000 from the twelve tribes of Israel should be taken as symbolic, especially since the tribe of Dan is not included. This is not a list of those who will be granted entrance into heaven, as though admission will somehow be limited to 144,000 even though billions and billions of people have lived on the earth since God first created Adam and Eve. This list and the promise it contains remind us that no matter what may happen, God will protect those who belong to him.

Revelation 8–11

Seven angels receive seven trumpets that unleash seven different judgments. Trumpets were used in the Bible as signals to the people, especially in times of war. In this case they signal that

God has declared war on sin, which means all sinners should repent. Revelation 9:20-21 reveals that in spite of the judgment raining down upon their heads, the people of the earth will refuse to turn away from their sin and toward God. Their stubbornness pushes God to the edge. He has delayed Christ's Second Coming to allow people to repent and be saved (2 Peter 3:15). When they don't turn away from sin even after all God has done, what choice does he have but to finally bring history to its conclusion?

Revelation 12–14

Chapter 12 tells of Satan's attempts to thwart God's plan of salvation, going back to the beginning of time. The woman is Israel, the dragon is Satan, and the child is Jesus. The chapter also shows how Satan's battles against God and his followers on this earth are a continuation of the rebellion he first launched in heaven.

Chapter 13 describes the coming of the Beast, or Antichrist, and his attempts to force the entire world to worship him. Because this chapter comes on the heels of chapter 12, we know his efforts will fail. His rebellion against God at the end of time will be as successful as all of Satan's schemes since the dawn of time. God always wins, and these chapters remind us he always will.

Revelation 15–17

These chapters describe the final three outpourings of God's wrath before Christ returns. The seven bowl judgments complete the process. Once again, people curse God rather than turn to him as his wrath is poured out. The "great prostitute" was most likely understood to represent Rome when John first penned these words.

Revelation 18–19

And now for the part we've been waiting for. History reaches its zenith on the day Jesus returns. He comes as a conquering King. All the armies of the world wait to fight against him, but it's not much of a battle. Just as he spoke all of creation into existence, he merely speaks, and the armies all fall down in defeat. This is the good news we long to see come true. Jesus will return. God wins in the end. Every trace of sin and its effects will be removed forever. This is the hope that drives us and gives us the grace to withstand anything we may face.

Revelation 20–22

My favorite part of John's description of heaven is 21:4. The NIV renders this verse, "He [God] will wipe every tear from their eyes." This is the heaven that awaits us. It isn't about the streets of gold and the gates made of giant pearls. The sweetest part of heaven lies in the relationship we will have with our God. Tender, merciful, but more than anything, face-to-face, we will finally be with the One we've loved from afar for so long.

Notes

Introduction

1. Stephen Baldwin in a personal interview with the author, October 13, 2005.

2. TH1NK's one-year Bible, *Pause*, uses this order.

3. Paul House, *Old Testament Survey* (Nashville: Broadman and Holman, 1992), 20–21.

Section 4: The Writings

1. J. A. Thompson, *The New American Commentary, 1, 2 Chronicles* (Nashville: Broadman, Holman), 1994, 49.

Section 5: The Good News

1. Walter Liefeld, "Luke," *The Expositor's Bible Commentary*, vol. 8 (Grand Rapids, MI: Zondervan, 1984), 861.

About the Author

MARK TABB is general editor of the TH1NK REFERENCE COLLECTION, as well as the author of twelve books, including *Living with Less* and *Greater Than: Unconventional Thoughts on the Infinite God*. He and his family live in Indiana with their two dachshunds.

About the Scholar Board

All books in the TH1NK REFERENCE COLLECTION have been reviewed for biblical accuracy by the following academic scholars:

Robert Don Hughes, PhD

professor of missions and evangelism, Clear Creek Baptist College, Pineville, Kentucky

Bob has a strong pastoral background as well as great strength as a writer. He knows people. He knows their needs. He is on this board to make sure these books speak to real people in the real world. In addition, he has impeccable academic qualifications and understands and works well with those from across the theological scale.

Jerry A. Johnson, PhD

president and professor of theology and ethics, The Criswell College, Dallas, Texas

Jerry has extensive expertise in the area of theology and worldviews. In addition to serving as president of The Criswell College and as a theology professor there, he has a daily radio program that focuses on applying a Christian worldview to every aspect of life.

Keith Reeves, PhD

professor of New Testament and early Christian literature in the School of Theology, Azusa Pacific University, Azusa, California

Keith brings a different perspective to the books, from both a theological and geographical standpoint. His views on the Bible and creation differ from the others on the scholar board. Also, the fact that he teaches in Southern California gives him a different perspective from both the writers of the first three books and the members of the board. In addition, Keith is an expert in New Testament and early Christian literature.

Joseph Thomas, PhD

assistant professor of church history, Biblical Seminary, Hatfield, Pennsylvania; director of Christian History Institute (CHI)

Joe combines a strong background in church history with a Wesleyan/Holiness theological background. Before pursuing his PhD, he taught history in a Christian high school for eight years, thereby developing a strong ability to communicate with our target audience.

GET THE FULL THINK STUDENT LIBRARY.

Theology

1-57683-957-5

Using a conversational approach and relevant mind-set, this unique guide will help students learn that theology can unite the body of Christ in truth and purpose.

Worldviews

1-57683-955-9

Worldviews is a quick-reference tool that equips students with a broad perspective on the various world beliefs and religions while comparing them to the Christian faith.